THE POWE
FROM

For Personal Happiness and Well-being

For Communities

Kath Reade

WMP

KATH READE

The Powerhouse of Meditation: From Stress to Vitality

Kath Reade

First published in October 2022

ISBN 978-1-914265-44-0 ebk

ISBN 978-1-914265-45-7 pbk

A CIP catalogue record for this book is available from the British Library.

Disclaimer: *The Powerhouse of Meditation: From Stress to Vitality* is intended for information and education purposes only. This book does not constitute specific legal, financial, health, clinical or commercial advice unique to your situation.

The views and opinions expressed in this book are those of the authors and do not reflect those of the Publisher and Resellers, who accept no responsibility for loss, damage or injury to persons or their belongings as a direct or indirect result of reading this book. All people mentioned in case studies have been used with permission, and/or have had names, genders, industries and personal details altered to protect client confidentiality.

Front Cover: The Zen Circle. An ancient one-stroke cailligraphy
symbolising who we truly are in our beautiful imperfection.

CONTENTS

DEDICATION

I dedicate this book with a deep bow of gratitude to:

- My dear husband Paul for his love and support.
- My dearly loved son Shaun, a constant inspiration.
- Ajahn Brahm, the Abbot of Bodhinyana Monastery in Serpentine, WA, (1995 to present) and the Spiritual Director of the Buddhist Society of Western Australia (1995 to present). His talks and meditations have been a mainstay of my practice over many years.
- Master Zhixing Wang. Words cannot express his power and mastery of Qi Gong and the benefits I have derived from his kind teachings.
- Deva Premal and Miten for their devotional music.
- Dent Meditation Centre in the Yorkshire Dales National Park, where I trained as a meditation teacher.
- Gaia House Retreat Centre in Devon, UK., where I have spent so many life-enhancing silent retreats.
- My treasured friends for their loving support and encouragement.
- To all who have attended my meditation groups in person and online.
- To Jack Kornfield whose books on meditation were an early invaluable influence to which I regularly return.
- To Joni Mitchell, Aretha Franklin, Ella Fitzgerald, and Maya Angelou whose music and poetry are in my soul.

WELCOME

This book is offered as a meditation. I invite you to read in this spirit. Let the words wash over you and sense their effect. The words are chosen to be meditative, calming, and energising as you read.

The book offers you the opportunity to establish your own daily meditation practice to reap untold benefits to your health and well-being, your relationships, and success in your chosen path.

You will find your meditation practice ultimately deeply moving, touching, beautiful and profound. The joys of life in the present moment will be revealed. There may be tears along the way but if so, they will be those that need to be shed, to make you lighter, and freer.

As you relax, restore, and reach for your dreams, you will know happiness beyond material possessions, the bliss of knowing you are enough, the peace of knowing your authentic self. You will cultivate the kindness and compassion that will transform your life.

THE CALM TEST

How calm are you now?

Pause for a few moments, close your eyes, and ask yourself, 'How calm do I feel right now?' Choose one of these words to describe your current state of being:

a) Very calm

b) Calm

c) Slightly calm

d) Not calm

e) Agitated

f) Slightly stressed

g) Stressed

h) Very stressed.

This book offers you ways to explore the path to greater inner peace and joy to live your best, most creative life. By establishing your meditation practice you may come to consistently score a), b), or c). Meditation cannot be underestimated in what it can do for us, so you can take this test again at the end of the book, or after you have been meditating regularly, and see how your 'calm status' may have changed.

CHAPTER ONE

HAPPINESS IN THE PRESENT MOMENT

Meditation is not an intellectual exercise. It is an experience. To get the proven great benefits you have to devote some time and commitment to the practice of meditation. This will be some of the most worthwhile time you have ever invested in your well-being.

To still the body, calm the mind, and cultivate compassion is to build the bedrock from which the fountain of your energy and creativity will joyfully flow.

Taking your meditation seat

The practice of sitting in silence and stillness can reveal profound truths about how to live your life in happiness. You can research the subject of meditation, and become knowledgeable, and you can join a group with a meditation teacher, but it is in the regular, disciplined practice of meditating, in the present moment, that the benefits will develop. For these benefits are cumulative. If you practice regularly, then over time you will become less stressed, less angry, less sad, less frustrated. You will find the keys to being happier, kinder, more peaceful, and more fulfilled.

Ajahn Brahm tells this story. A little girl heard her mother say that she would give her meditation class a miss this evening and she asked, 'But why Mummy?'

'Because I don't have time', replied her mother.

'Mummy please go to meditation,' urged her young daughter.

Her mother was puzzled. 'Why darling?'

The little girl replied, 'Because you are a nicer mummy when you have been to meditation.'

Find Your Calm, Find Your Courage

The image of the meditator as still and serene is only half the story. The calming effect of meditation can clear your way to being fully energised and able to be creative. In meditation a great deal of stress and worry, or past trauma, can arise in a pure form and eventually dissipate. It requires you to stay with it. Meditation reduces stress and creates spaciousness in your mind and being. You will find more courage to take the path in life that is waiting for you if you find the courage to stick with meditation.

The question in meditation is always: *Can you be with it?*

If the answer is: Yes, I can be with it, then you will go from strength to strength in your life.

Dynamic action is the natural consequence of the space that meditation creates as it dissolves the debris of our stored negativity and hurt. If compassion and kindness have been cultivated as an integral part of meditation, then the dynamic action will be rightfully directed for the good of yourself and all beings. The cultivation of patience is invaluable to increase your assertiveness. You will be more able to stand up for yourself to take your place in the world.

Meditation can be the powerhouse and the foundation of you achieving your aims. In the 1940s, Gandhi led the Indian people to the liberation of India from British colonial rule by peaceful non-violent action fuelled from the wellspring of his daily morning meditation.

In modern times many CEOs of major businesses thank meditation. Billionaire Marc Benioff CEO of SalesForce, a company worth $97 billion, credits meditation for his leadership style and has meditation rooms throughout his company. Paul McCartney says, 'In moments of madness, meditation has helped me find moments of serenity.'

Oprah Winfrey has championed meditation globally in partnership with teachers Eckhart Tolle and Deepak Chopra. She has often spoken of the importance of meditation to stay connected with your authentic self, especially when all around you is frenetic.

Meditation can be your inspiration whether you want to have a rich spiritual life, or be a successful business entrepreneur, live a creative life, or lead a life of service to others. Essentially, whatever your path, meditation will enhance the quality of your life.

It can appear that meditation is passive but in fact it can often inspire action. After decades of meditation in monastic life, the Buddhist monk Ajahn Brahm stood up assertively, but peacefully, for the right of women to be ordained as Buddhist nuns in 2009. He encountered great opposition and censure, lost friends, and had to find steadfastness and courage to see it through, which he courageously did. Meditation can be a firm foundation for right speech and right action when required. It is dynamic, it is inspirational, it is ethical, it is about integrity of body, mind, and spirit. It is also about building inner strength and the resilience to ride out the storms that come into your life. Meditation can free your creativity to soar and succeed in your chosen field of endeavour. It is, above all, about kindness and compassion, towards yourself, and towards others.

Who Is This Book For?

This book is intended for you, whether you are an experienced meditator, a beginner, or curious. For it is about simple truths that need to be refreshed and reviewed regularly.

The saying goes, 'In the eyes of the expert the possibilities are few but in the eyes of the beginner they are endless.'

I encourage readers of all degrees of experience and none to approach meditation with the beginner's mind.

What Is Meditation?

In essence, we still the body, calm the mind, follow the breath. We discover the transformational power of the gift of silence. It is the practice of listening deeply, to gain insight, wisdom, and peace in our hearts.

Meditation is the practice of staying in the present moment for a sustained period of time. It requires you to let go of your past, all of it, in the now of this meditation. It has no place right here, right now, in this moment. All the history of your life so far can be swept aside and let go of in your meditation. All you need to experience is the purity and clarity of this present moment. It is here that peace dwells.

It is also letting go of the future. The plans, the anticipations. Experience shows us that we cannot know what the future holds, so we drop it, abandon it, let it go during the meditation. Do not necessarily expect instant achievement of this, but set the intention, for it is possible to cultivate, train your mind to be able to do so.

If we persevere in letting go of the two great burdens of past and future, for the duration of the meditation, we will be able to sustain a period of being in the present moment and this is the first ingredient of arriving at joy and inner peace.

As we sit and let go of thoughts about the past and the future, just for the moment at least, we begin to be able to live more fully in the present moment. This is tremendously uplifting to your soul and liberating for your mind and body.

We allow our worries and anxieties to fall away for now, for this meditation. We become more present, more still in our body, calmer in our minds. We feel kindness towards ourselves and others as an intention and a practice.

Can We Enjoy Our Meditation?

Yes, it can be so delightful. We can delight in relaxing the body first, then the mind, and reach a joyful state of being. It is powerful to make the intention to relax and enjoy the meditation. It is not intended to be physically painful nor for the meditation to be an internal war of 'trying' to force oneself to concentrate. If this is happening, let go and declare peace within. Adjust your posture to be more comfortable.

THE PRACTICE

It is helpful to see meditation as having three stages. Still the body. Calm the mind. Follow the breath.

STILL THE BODY

I encourage you to take time to allow this relaxation by bringing loving attention to your whole body, part by part, from the toes up to the top of your head. Intend this to be enjoyable and so good for you. With proper attention we can identify any areas of discomfort or pain and envelope these areas with loving kindness. Do not underestimate the healing effect of this on your body and give some time to this important piece of self-care. Only when you feel more relaxed in the body do you feel ready to bring your attention to the mind. Use the body scan meditation as a beautiful way to encourage complete physical relaxation.

THE BODY SCAN MEDITATION

Sit in a comfortable yet erect posture with the dignity of a king or queen. Feel where your body connects to the earth. Rest your hands comfortably on your lap.

Feel a sense of kindness towards your body throughout this exercise. Bring lots of loving kindness to any pain-filled areas. This can have a soothing and healing effect. Do this body scan meditation very slowly and in the spirit of allowing and letting go for the best effect.

Bring your awareness to the soles of your feet and relax them including your big toes and all the rest of your toes.

Now become aware of the tops of your feet and then relax your heels and your ankles.

Relax your calf muscles and the front of your lower legs. Bring your awareness to your knees, relax the kneecaps and the ligaments.

Travel your awareness to your thighs and the backs of your thighs, and to your buttocks.

Let any tension relax from your muscles.

Become aware of your *Lower Dan Tian*, the Chinese medicine description for the energetic centre below your navel. At the width of two fingers inward imagine there is a spinning pearl of light. You can always return to holding your awareness of this area energetically speaking, to build up your life force energy. Here is the seat of your creativity.

Bring relaxation to your lower back, travelling up to the kidneys, and letting go of any fear stored there.

Now travel around to your lower digestive tract, and then to your liver and spleen area. Relax these organs kindly and let go of any anger stored here.

Become aware of your stomach and let it relax, before slowly travelling to the lungs.

Relax your lungs and bring loving kindness to them allowing any grief, sadness, or sorrow to dissipate through the out- breath.

Bring your awareness to your heart area, the centre of love, and in some cases deep hurt also. Bring your loving kindness and compassion to rest here for a few moments.

Take your awareness to your throat and let the muscles of your throat relax.

Relax your shoulders where a lot of tension is often felt, along with the back of your neck.

Relax your right arm, elbow, wrist hand, thumb, and fingers. Relax your left arm, elbow, wrist, thumb, and fingers.

Travel back along your arms up to the ears and relax the inner and outer ears. Bring loving kindness to your brain and nourish your precious control centre with gratitude.

Now relax your scalp and the roots of your hair.

Let the muscles around your eyes relax. Let your eyes be soft.

Bring your awareness to your jaw and let these muscles relax and soften. Your tongue and your lips can also relax from the mask of everyday life.

Let any remaining tension anywhere in your body be washed away into the earth as you imagine a warm, golden fountain cascading gently over your head and body.

Now simply sit in silence and stillness for a few minutes.

CALM THE MIND

When we have given sufficient attention to relaxing our body, our mind is more likely to be able to just naturally follow the breath. After all, we are continuing to breath automatically anyway, so the breath will come up naturally, and we can simply enjoy the process, by becoming more aware.

Make an intention to enjoy this precious opportunity to meditate.

Having firstly stilled the body, and secondly calmed the mind, it is then possible to go deeper and deeper into an enjoyable state of joy and bliss. It is most important not to seek after this state, but to simply adopt the techniques of meditation, practice regularly, and accept what comes.

Meditations vary a great deal from day to day. Take it all, take the rough with the smooth. You will benefit by opening your heart and mind to what lessons and insights may be revealed.

Meditation is like the landscape of the earth, with constant variety and constant change, and you learn to just be there for it all on your meditation journey. It can all eventually be taken in your stride if you have the right equipment to cope with it, in this case the techniques of meditation and the soul of compassion.

There are the mountains of high exhilarations, and the deep dark forests of despair. There can be seemingly endless, boring plains and deserts, and the deep joy of floating on a calm blue sea watching the sky.

Experience it all with balance and equanimity in the sure knowledge nothing lasts for ever.

Let go of attachment to outcome so you can be free and open to whatever arises. This requires your willingness to countenance letting go of your attachment to following your thoughts wherever they lead.

We allow thoughts and feelings to come, be, and go on by, like passing clouds across the sky. We begin to realise that we are not our thoughts and we become witness to our crazy monkey mind rather than the prisoner of it. We now understand that we do not have to follow every thought that pops unbidden into our mind and we can return our awareness to our breath.

We discover that there is a larger consciousness that we become aware of. Even beyond the name we currently have. With this expanded consciousness comes the wonderful spaciousness which frees up our mind. We go beyond the 'I' of 'I am'.

Instead of holding on to the constant baggage of thoughts cluttering our mind we develop the skill of letting go of these. As we develop the realisation that we do not have to follow every thought that comes up, we begin to feel lighter and can gain the freedom to go deeper into the meditation. Practice this and let go of expectations of higher states of bliss. This is the skill of letting go and thereby going deep, eventually into bliss. Forget and abandon any desire for, or attachment to bliss in favour of staying in the present moment and letting go. This is the practice that will deliver joy and bliss without seeking them.

FOLLOW THE BREATH

After stilling the body and calming the mind, you can progress to placing your awareness on your breath. Carefully observe your in-breath and your out-breath without changing or judging it, just as it is. If your mind begins to wander, bring your awareness back to watch your in- breath and your out- breath without frustration or irritation, but with kindness towards yourself.

There are many methods of following the breath. One is to count your breaths on each in-breath which helps to keep your focus. Try this now to 20 breaths.

You can begin to notice the space between the in-breath and the out-breath, and the space between the out-breath and the next in-breath, just as it is, without changing it. Just relax and sense the effect.

Ultimately it is very beneficial to be able to count one hundred breaths with full concentration, fully in the present moment. Counting is only one of many ways to follow the breath.

What may at first seem a difficult and challenging process becomes a skill which delivers the great beauty of the now to you. It is a rewarding practice which will birth great calm deep in your inner being.

The peace and calm that gradually grows in your heart, and your whole being, as you regularly meditate comes from learning about how to be, developing the ability to simply be, here and now. It comes from letting go and just being. We sit in a comfortable but erect and dignified position and rest there, quietly, letting all things arise and all things pass. For sooner or later, they do.

We soften our eyes, and our heart, and just notice the breath. The in breath, the out breath, just as it is, without changing it. Awareness of our breath can be our anchor that we return to time and time again when the kites of our thoughts have flown our mind away again.

Return to the breath a thousand times and a thousand times you will be blessed. This is the practice so please, never chastise yourself when your mind wanders. Just return to the anchor of your breath without judgment. This is the way of kindness meditation.

MEDITATING REGULARLY

We make this a regular, even daily practice. We notice the increasing effects of this meditation practice as our level of inner calm accumulates. You can keep a journal of your progress if you wish to see how far you have come. You will notice the difference and realise you now have tools to deal with stress, worry, and being stuck in past experiences, or concerns about the future.

This is an ideal and very manageable way to begin to establish your daily meditation practice.

FIND YOUR MEDITATION POWER SPOT

I encourage you to experiment with finding the best position and place in your home or garden to sit for your regular meditation time. You can benefit by making this your regular power spot, the place you have your meditation seat, cushion, or chair, and even a small altar if wished. Try to make it a pleasant spot which is easy for you to think about spending time in, and which has the right ambience for you to want to sit there.

You may want to have your favourite blanket or jacket there to keep warm and you may like to light a candle or have a meditation figure or some treasured photo, flowers, or crystals in the room. This is up to you.

I have a seated Buddha figure because of her tranquil expression. Meditation is not the sole province of any religion or philosophy but can be part of any or none. It is however an ethical practice, encouraging us to respect the sanctity of all living beings, and our planet.

MEDITATION POSTURES

There are many possible postures, sitting, lying down, standing, and walking slowly. All are acceptable and a matter of choice. The common requirements are to have a straight back but not strained, with the head aligned with the spine. Your hands rest together in your lap, or separately on the legs.

Sitting cross-legged on the floor a cushion is used to support your spine, so your knees are lower than your sitting bones. You may be more comfortable with further cushions under your knees or ankles but do experiment.

You may wish to sit on a chair. There is no requirement to be in pain in your meditation posture, so develop a posture which supports the alert relaxation you are cultivating. Be mindful of your body's comfort and do adjust your position if you develop numbness or unbearable pain. This will support you to be able to stay in position to meditate. There are many kinds of meditation cushions and stools available to support your practice.

If you prefer a chair, preferably sit on the first third of the chair rather than leaning on the back. Your posture ideally should be upright with both feet on the floor and hands resting on your lap. Keep your spine straight and shoulders back and relaxed. Keep your head erect and look ahead with a soft gaze.

Then gently close your eyes to meditate.

If for any reason some postures present difficulties for you then you can lay on your back on the floor. Usually, you lay on a yoga mat with your toes pointed slightly outward and your palms facing up, but the most important thing is to develop a posture that is comfortable enough for you to sustain so do minimise any discomfort and follow the principle of being kind to yourself.

You may benefit from a cushion placed under the knees and feet flat to the floor, or a flat one placed under the neck and head. Do experiment but bear in mind there can be a tendency to fall asleep lying down.

You usually close your eyes to meditate, and open them at the end of the meditation, keeping your eyes soft and gentle. You can sometimes practice with half open or open eyes possibly gazing at an object too.

You are encouraged to make a connection through your feet to the earth and you can imagine a golden cord along your spine connecting the top of your head with the universal energy source. In this way you rest, perfectly balanced between the grounding earth and the cosmic universal energy.

LENGTH OF MEDITATION

Ideally a meditation session will be of more benefit if it can last an hour or even longer, but any lesser amount of time is fine and beneficial. You can begin with five minutes a day, then fifteen, thirty, and then forty-five minutes of sitting meditation.

If you can meditate for fifteen minutes every day you will notice your gradual transformation to more calm and inner peace.

It is possible to develop the ability to return to your inner peace within amid any situation just to regain your equilibrium. We can return to an awareness of our breath, even briefly.

The old adage of counting to ten to prevent yourself flying off the handle is quite wise. Combine this with a few deeper breaths and letting your shoulders go down a few notches too for an instant calming effect.

MY YOU TUBE FREE 14-DAY COURSE OF SHORT MEDITATIONS TO ESTABLISH A DAILY PRACTICE

As a compendium to this book, I recommend you watch my fourteen daily short meditations: *https://bit.ly/3DXrvVD*

Search YouTube for playlist headed:

Kath Reade Five Minute Meditations

CHAPTER TWO

KIND MINDFULNESS AND OVERCOMING DIFFICULTIES

Mindfulness is a meditation technique to train the mind to be fully in the present moment and can be practised at any point through daily life.

We so often completely miss the present moment. The wonders of what is in the now can be obscured by all sorts of distractions.

Maybe we are busy evaluating what went on recently or in the distant past and feeling a variety of emotions associated with those thoughts. We may get caught up in the planning mind.

We may often be on autopilot in the now. For example. We may be walking in beautiful countryside but because we are talking about something that happened to us, we are completely unaware of the gorgeous view, the hills, the lake with its sunlit ripples.

You will be able to recall times when you have suddenly become aware of your surroundings and realised you have not been present, but rather lost in thought or animated talking.

Mindfulness is the technique of consciously staying aware of what is happening in the now and fully appreciating the present moment experience whatever you are doing and wherever you are.

So if you are walking in a wood you are being mindful of each step and aware of how the ground feels to your feet. You will see the trees and be aware of their life and vibrancy, their shapes, their colours.

You will be observing how that makes you feel. You will hear the birdsong and smell the vegetation and the woodland air. You will be fully aware and present in the experience of the wood instead of mindlessly, blindly, deafly walking through and missing everything in the here and now.

A helpful technique is to look at something on your walk and ask yourself three questions:

What is it?

What is it doing?

How does it make you feel?

Here is an example of this noticing technique from my experience on a walk in the Yorkshire Dales:

In the deep mossed old stone trough,

The water rests and gently ripples.

Remembering the caress

Of many a horse's thirsty lip.

My heart feels the flow of time.

If you carry a small notebook, you can practice mindfully noticing. You can pause and write some lines about your present experience.

As you practice mindfulness in your day-to-day activities at work and play, your mind becomes more disciplined, more aware. You will discover a greater clarity of mind, a greater appreciation of the beautiful aspects of the present moment, and an enriched existence.

When you are walking, just walk. When you are cooking, just cook. When you listen, wholeheartedly listen. When you are making a cup of tea just make the cup of tea, and when you drink it, just drink it - tasting every sip to the full, being aware of the warm liquid in your mouth and flowing into your stomach.

Be fully here, now.

THE MINDFULNESS RAISIN EXERCISE

To get a sense of this way of being, take one raisin. Roll it gently between your finger and thumb and fully experience its shape, colour, and texture. Place it in your mouth and allow your tongue to explore the taste and feel of the raisin.

Think with gratitude of all that contributed to this raisin being here, now. The earth in which the vines grow, the sun that ripened them, the water that nourished them and all the workers that tended them.

There is no need to rush to bite through the raisin but when you do, be aware of how your teeth do this and how your tongue works with the roof of your mouth to taste the flavour. Observe the process of saliva coming to deal with the raisin and fully enjoy the feel and flavour. Continue your mindful awareness through swallowing.

The raisin experiment is an insight into just how much of the present moment we usually miss as we rush on from one thing to another.

WALKING MEDITATION

Now we can apply this mindful approach to walking with great benefits to our calm and our appreciation of being in the now.

The method is to bring your awareness to very slow and deliberate walking steps. You may do this in the open air or wherever you can choose a distance of about fifteen feet or four to five metres.

Walk very slowly up and down this distance being mindfully aware of the way your heel slowly leaves the ground first, followed by your foot and toes. Feel the muscles and tendons working to lift your leg and slowly bring it down to the ground heel first with the toes following. Continue to walk in this mindful way for fifteen minutes or so, and then sit and sense the effect.

If you are in nature, you will often find your peaceful awareness becomes so alive to the apprehension of colours and shapes of leaves and trees. You may be alive in a more intense way to the beauty of surroundings. You may gaze at the veins in a leaf and see their miracle in a way you had not often done.

You may feel more at peace, and this can be a wonderful connection to your creativity and your energy.

Mindfulness techniques are used to reduce stress and there are proven results in research done since the 1960s when Jon Kabat-Zin developed his *Mindfulness Based Stress Reduction* approach.

In truth he was drawing on traditions stretching back for thousands of years. This has become very popular as a way of managing stress, in the workplace, in mental health and in many settings. This approach does not emphasise ethical living. You could even say it is a technique which is effective but by itself could be morally neutral. Therefore, traditionally the cultivation of kindness and compassion is also an indispensable part of meditation.

KINDNESS AND COMPASSION

The Dalai Lama has spoken of the core qualities of meditation being *Kindness* and *Compassion.* These tend to grow in people who practice meditation regularly. Stress reduction is also highly desirable to become a healthy functioning person, but meditation goes further in being dedicated to revealing and strengthening the true compassionate nature of beings. This usually leads to greater compassion towards oneself and towards others.

The benefits of these ethical qualities to peace and loving kindness between people cannot be overestimated.

Mindfulness plus Kindness is the ideal formula to bring together technique and ethical foundation. The application of kindness starts with truly taking time to apply it to yourself, often.

COMMON OBSTACLES TO MEDITATION

The early Buddhist ancient texts identified hindrances to meditation that tend to arise in all of us. It can help to know you are not the only one facing these difficulties. It is illuminating to identify and examine them. We can consider approaches to deal with hindrances, once aware of them.

As you sit in meditation with your awareness on your breath you may, sooner or later, experience the common feelings that arise and hinder you.

Welcome them all as your teachers.

ANGER

When anger comes up, it is helpful to name it and examine what it is, how it makes you feel, and notice how long it lasts. Under this gaze, the anger will gradually fade or change. We will eventually realise we do not need to fear this feeling for it does not last at the same level of intensity, especially if we have the intention to let it be, acknowledge it, and let it go.

We stay in the sanctuary of the in breath and the out breath and all will pass. Maybe not easily, maybe not straight away, but trust this process, and results will be seen.

WANTING

As we sit, desires and the wanting mind often arise to distract us from peace within. We name these desires and examine them. We breath into them. How does it feel in the body, in the mind, to grasp after something we want? Can we stay with this feeling until it begins to subside?

This is what dissatisfaction feels like, a part of the human condition. However, it is not an inevitability, and can be counteracted. Stay with it, witness it, and you will gain the great insight that *THIS TOO SHALL PASS.*

So much relief comes to the soul and relaxation of our tense body when we diminish our wanting of things.

FEELING SLEEPY

One of our most common obstacles to reaping the benefits of meditation is sleepiness. When we stop rushing about and deliberately sit down and do nothing, we may feel drowsy quite quickly. When this happens, it reveals to us how tired we are.

The closing of our eyes, the relaxation of our body, and the calming of our mind may bring our breath to be deeper and longer. Before long, our head may begin to loll. When you return to consciousness, notice and name it. Examine its nature and you may realise you genuinely need more sleep. Especially if you apply kindness to yourself and your needs. Please do not judge yourself harshly as this is counterproductive to the benefits of meditation.

Meditation is all about awakening. It is about being able to somewhat detach, and watch your feelings and thoughts, rather than being like an autumn leaf being whirled hither and thither by strong winds.

Sleep can also be a form of avoidance. For when we meditate, we come face to face with ourselves. Again, bring loving kindness curiosity to your experience during meditation to attain greater insight and understanding. If you do this, you will increase your wisdom and in time the quality of your meditation with all the benefits this will bring to your life.

FEAR

We may notice a feeling of fear arising. Name this too and examine its characteristics.

This may not always be comfortable and so it can be preferable to escape into sleep. Notice if this is happening.

Try not to be self-critical but simply observe these obstacles, bring kind understanding and tolerance to them. Be patient. There will be a good reason why your fear or anger lives within and sometimes arises. It always deserves your compassion. In time you can learn to relax into it and begin to let it go when it is ready to go.

DOUBT

Doubt is a difficulty that can dog our quicksilver minds. We may doubt the process or value of meditation or doubt our own abilities. We may range over things we did or did not do in our lives.

Sit and watch these doubts, stay with them as you would watch a tree blown around by strong winds. The winds of doubt will subside, and the tree will become still and peaceful again, as will you with your compassionate attention and perseverance. Become aware of the tree-roots grounding you and know you can be flexible and strong to endure difficulties.

TRUST THE PROCESS

The experience over thousands of years of meditation is that the technique of patient naming of difficulties and staying with them, has the effect that they all eventually transform and dissolve. Our inner peace will deepen in the process. Essentially, we apply self-compassion and kindness. We come to trust this process as we discover for ourselves that:

ALL THINGS ARISE AND ALL THINGS PASS

We come to rest in this truth. Meditation becomes our refuge. We dissolve stress and recharge our batteries.

DOING YOUR BEST IS ENOUGH

To be both realistic and kind is to accept that we will of course experience these hindrances even when we become regular meditators from time to time. The important thing is that we are able to be aware and wiser about them, and we have the tools to deal with them. So we notice when and what feelings are arising and we consciously decide to ride them out by being with what arises, and bringing loving kindness to ourselves as we focus again on the anchor of the breath.

Dealing with difficulties experienced in meditation brings up the question centre stage. What were we expecting? Often suffering and dissatisfaction arises when reality does not tally with our expectations. We can experiment with dropping the wanting, the desire for a 'better' meditation. We can drop the fault-finding mind, which can become a negative masochistic habit of mind. We can smile and even laugh at our situation and how we are dealing with it.

We can set an intention to simply drop becoming upset and self-critical or critical of others. We can use our techniques to encourage our mind and body to relax. We can make peace within.

We know that when we experience difficulties, that is the time we can learn.

CHAPTER THREE

LIBERATING THE MIND FOR DYNAMIC RESULTS

SUSPENDING JUDGMENT

We can cling to making judgments and holding strong opinions as a way of giving ourselves some sort of certainty in an uncertain world. This can serve to close our eyes and hearts and shut down many other possibilities. Events and people may not always be as they seem. If we do not cloud our eyes with judgments, we may begin to see the true nature of things with more clarity and insight.

An example would be when you take a strong dislike to someone, but on getting to know them better you discover the difficult life they have had. Your heart softens and you find you have a lot more tolerance for that person.

There are many Buddhist stories stretching back into antiquity which beautifully illustrate life lessons. The one about the folly of rushing to judgment goes thus:

A farmer lost his horse one day when it ran away, and his friends all said, ‘Oh no! what bad luck!’

The farmer replied, ‘Maybe, maybe not.’ The next day his horse returned, bringing three wild horses with it.

‘Well, that’s marvellous!’ exclaimed his friends.

‘Maybe.’ replied the farmer.

Next day the farmer’s son rode one of the wild horses, which threw him, and his son's leg was broken. Once again, the farmer's friends sympathised on this bad luck.

'Maybe.' said the farmer.

Soon after, the military came to the village and took all the young men for the army. They did not take the farmer's son because of his broken leg. His friends were congratulating him on his good luck when the farmer remarked, 'Maybe.'

Life is unpredictable which is a reason to make the most of the present moment and find happiness in it without making snap judgments about how life may unfold. Can you follow a practice of non-judgment for a while as an experiment?

EMPATHY

We may temper our rush to judgments by attempting to put ourselves in the other persons shoes. The ability to be able to understand and feel how another person may feel is a key skill.

In my early days of learning to meditate, we were encouraged by teachers to let go of judgments and opinions as an exercise in developing more understanding and kindness.

This was a liberating experience, and I encourage you to try it for a few days. Instead of jumping in to give your opinion, you will become a better listener and often, learn more. It is in fact a relief at times and an enlightening exercise. You will find your meditations becoming deeper, kinder, and more peaceful. You will delight in the peace you are cultivating. A meditation teacher once suggested that we should look upon another person as if they were our son or daughter to develop more compassionate listening. It is amazing how effective this technique can be in finding empathy rather than irritation towards another being.

RESTLESSNESS AND AGITATION

It is important to accept that you are not always in the same mental and physical state of being each day when you come to your meditation seat. This too we accept as something to be noticed, witnessed, and named as we breathe our way gently through.

One day we may begin to meditate only to notice that our mind is in the grip of anxiety and worry. Or our body may be constantly uncomfortable and fidgeting. Sometimes this will settle but there may be days when we are drawn into a struggle in our minds or bodies.

We can spend the whole meditation struggling to control our thoughts so that we can subdue our anxiety.

This is like an internal conflict but once we bring mindful attention to this state, we can drop our struggling. We begin to watch our worries as we would watch a stormy sky. We start to be able to realise, we are not our thoughts. We watch our thoughts from our deeper consciousness as they arise, appearing and disappearing, one after the other.

Sometimes they are short-lived but sometimes they are more resistant and stay longer. We may stand up and feel that was not a great meditation overall. However, there are no failed meditations, only opportunities for greater insight and awareness.

Another day we sit in our meditation spot and relax our bodies bit by bit, and calm our minds, putting our attention on our breath or on our feet on the earth, and we may have a beautiful meditation which leaves us feeling joy, bliss, and contentment.

We come to realise this is the way of all life, the ups and downs, and the variations over time. All part of life's rich pattern.

Please consider there are no bad meditations for they all have something to teach.

If you do not let the restless times put you off, and you continue with your practice, you will be rewarded with a growing sense of inner peace, a growing emotional resilience, and a sense that there is truly a place you can go to inside yourself at any time to connect with peacefulness. This inner peace temple is a place inside yourself that you can cultivate over time with regular meditation practice. Do not strive for it but allow it by letting go of the desire to control and staying with meditation practice.

IMPERMANENCE

We can rest amongst the chaos, the circumstances, and the conditions in ourselves and in all of life in the knowledge that nothing lasts. All is impermanent and this is the nature of all phenomena.

Nature and its seasons teach so much about the inevitability of constant change. Of birth, of vibrancy and strength, of decline and death. Of rebirth, and so on.

We bring mindful attention to the nature of existence and learn to be at peace in letting go of clinging on to that which cannot stay the same for ever.

There is a practice in Thailand of 'corpse meditation' by monks who observe over time, in meditation beside a dead body, the changes of decay. This is to understand the impermanence of the external body of a person. To see it is that person no longer. They have left their body. It brings the realisation that we need to make the most of mindful, kindful living in this short and precious life.

Clinging on to that which is by its nature constantly changing inevitably brings suffering said both the Buddha, and the ancient Greek philosophers. Impermanence and how to approach it features in both east and west philosophies.

The end of suffering lies in letting go of attachment and craving as we truly understand the nature of constant change of all things and lives.

Watch nature and impermanence. The tree does not rail against the autumn. It is in perfect harmony with its ever-changing cycles of change. It does not desire hopelessly to be permanently in bloom.

It fully lives in the moment and fully experiences life as it is, in the present. This is a wonderful lesson.

Watch a young child learning to walk. Baby steps, a cause of great joy for us to watch. Falling over, and banging her head, crying. A cause of suffering for us as we rush to pick her up and kiss her better. We beam with love as she continues tottering along. We see her heading towards the hot oven with fingers outstretched. A cause of great anxiety in us as we rush to save her from being burned. Later we beam with tranquillity and love as we watch her sleep. The constant change continues, and we realise the true nature of this impermanent world.

We make our peace with the true nature of this life.

We come to our meditation practice and cultivate these insights by staying with our breath and letting go of our cravings, and of our aversions. We set this intention. We smile.

As our meditations deepen over time the wonder is the growing compassion in our hearts for ourselves and for all beings. For all are impermanent, just as we are, and we have this in common.

We enjoy this present moment. How can we quarrel with other impermanent beings? How can we rush through life overlooking the beauty of silence, of the beautiful nature of the lake now coming to stillness like a great mirror, reflecting the slowly passing clouds?

Our job is simply to notice, to appreciate the present moment, to abandon all craving and to fully inhabit the now with a compassionate heart towards ourselves and all beings.

THE DYNAMIC RESULTS OF MEDITATION FOR YOUR LIFE

This is the practice. It is not passive. It is not opting out. It will unleash your creativity and you will have created the space to allow your life to blossom. You will be able to realise your talents and live your perceived purpose, underpinned by loving kindness. You will see the whole picture, the good, the bad, and the ugly, and embrace it all as the nature of existence.

You will simply do your best and it will, by definition, be enough.

Meditation will be your salvation, and the making of you, as it has been for me.

THE VALUE OF SILENCE

Silence is a gift. It is a respite from the need to keep talking or indeed listening to others. Only when you stop talking, making noise, do you realise what a precious thing silence is. Our soul yearns for silence sometimes, and only when we listen to our own heart, deeply, do we hear this. A meditation teacher said to one of her students who kept asking questions in a bid to further understand what she should be doing, 'Stop asking questions and all answers will eventually come in the silence. Silence answers everything.'

In the gift of silence, we make contact with how we really feel. We let go of the illusion that we can control what is going on. We realise how we are really feeling right now. As we stay in silence, we develop compassion eventually. We cease self-criticism, and self-acceptance becomes possible along with fully appreciating this present moment. A sense of refreshment, and inner peace is possible. It can be a much-needed rest for your mind. It is possible to discover, with delightful peace, the space between your in-breath and your out-breath as the perfect silence, the perfect pause, the perfect moment of peace.

We cannot expect everything around us in the world to become silent. That way lies frustration. It is you that is giving yourself the gift of silence within. Clarity, decision-making, concentration, compassion, energy, self-awareness, will all improve. Try also spending some time in silence with others and observe how profound and rewarding this can be. You can benefit from silence for a few minutes or on a week-long silent retreat. As long or as short as you can manage, the pause into silence will enrich you.

MEDITATION MAKES YOU HAPPIER AND HEALTHIER THE PROVEN BENEFITS:

Reduces stress

Controls anxiety

Improves emotional health

Enhances self-awareness

Lengthens attention span

May reduce age-related memory loss

Can generate kindness

May help with addictions

Improves sleep

Helps control pain

Can lower blood pressure

You can meditate anywhere, any time.

(From '12 Science-based Benefits of Meditation' by Thorpe and Link, medically reviewed by M. White Ph.D., MS, Psychology. Updated 27th October 2020. Reproduced in www.healthline.com)

FREQUENTLY ASKED QUESTIONS

Q. How can I stop myself from thinking when meditating?

A. Stop trying to and come back to following the breath or focus on your feet, time and time again. Detach somewhat from following your thoughts as they arise and pass.

Q. How can I learn more about meditation?

A. By meditating firstly. If you want to learn more, you could begin by reading about the teachings of the Buddha. Start with studying The Four Noble Truths.

They are:

The truth of suffering,

The truth of the cause of suffering,

The truth of the end of suffering, and

The truth of the path that leads to the end of suffering.

Q. How can I deal with thoughts if they distract me?

A. To realise you are not your thoughts and connect again with relaxing your body and coming to follow your breath. You do not have to follow or believe every thought but can gently return to your anchor be it the breath or awareness of your feet on the earth. We are not trying to stop thoughts, but we are noticing the thoughts and letting them go so that we do not get 'lost in thought'. The idea of your anchor in meditation is important to deal with thinking. You can return to it again and again.

That is the process.

CHAPTER FOUR

A RANGE OF POWERFUL WAYS TO MEDITATE

AWAKENING TO WHAT IS

You are no longer driven and defined by your ego. You no longer focus on the past and the future but now fully live in the present moment, the only one we ever truly have. You see and feel the connection between yourself and the world. You are the grain of sand, but you now see you are also the whole beach. You are both the cloud and the whole sky. Both the wave and the whole ocean.

NOTICING

You begin to give yourself time and space through meditation to notice all phenomena. You notice how you are feeling. You are fully here, now.

INSIGHT

The time and space to notice gives rise to insights about the truths of existence. You realise the limitations of chatter and busyness. A deep joy grows in you which becomes more consistent as you practice meditation. Meditation becomes more of a living delight than a chore or an internal war.

Inner peace grows and thus you become more able to live the life you were given with more energy, kindness, joy, and creativity.

You can rest fully and get a good night's sleep. Stress will have less and less of a hold over your life. Your physical health and mental well-being will improve.

This is the magical quality of silence and stillness, and of developing the ability to let go of that which we cling to. To let go of both wanting and not wanting.

Our awakened being will be a gradual joyful revelation to our spirit, body, and mind.

By becoming aware of the bigger picture, we are less likely to get caught up in petty irritations. We become calm and reflective like a clear still lake. We can ride change and the seasons of our life with greater equanimity.

We may become able to decide to look at our phone less and have times off social media. This will allow our brains to relax, restore, recharge. The scrolling habit is insidious, and we will benefit greatly from breaks from it, even if we decide not to look at it when we go to bed and when we rise, for a while. If you find that difficult, this is a sign that you will feel much better for a break from constant engagement with social media.

CONNECTING WITH YOUR LIFE FORCE ENERGY

As a result of awakening through meditation, your release of stress leads to a more relaxed body and mind. This liberates your creativity and builds your vitality.

Here are meditations based on these awakening principles to practice when you are irritated, frustrated, angry.

MOVEMENT MEDITATIONS
FOR WHEN YOU FEEL IRRITATED, FRUSTRATED, OR ANGRY

Anger floods our bodies with stress hormones. If we are often getting angry and stressed, this can lead to health problems such as digestive conditions, headaches, and many others. After anger, depression can follow as we turn the anger in on ourselves.

Meditation, both still and moving forms, can be a tremendous help to regaining your inner balance and sense of peace and tranquillity.

Let us suppose you have just become angry and frustrated in an argument. It is beneficial to go outside and take some deeper breaths, preferably near to trees and nature. Feel the coolness of the air coming into your nostrils as you take three deeper breaths in through your nose and out through your mouth.

Now shake your body just like a wet dog would shake after swimming in a lake. Do this for as long as you want. Shaking is a Qi Gong technique for galvanising energy and letting stale energy go.

Shake your head, your shoulders, arms, and hands.

Let your arms limply swing from the shoulders.

Shake your hips and each leg in turn.

Now come to rest in a standing position and imagine all the stress and irritation has been shaken loose and is now tumbling down through your body like iron filings, down through the soles of your feet into the earth.

Come to stillness standing with your feet planted on the ground, and imagine you are in a position slightly resembling being seated on a horse so that your body is not strained and can stand for some time:

Your knees slightly bent.

Your feet shoulder-width apart.

Your lower back relaxed.

Your shoulders relaxed.

Your neck relaxed and your head as though attached by a golden cord to the heavens.

Your arms hanging loosely by your side as if a tiny ball of air is under each arm pit.

Soften your eyes to a gentle gaze towards the horizon.

Stand like this for a couple of minutes.

Breath out the toxins of anger and frustration. Just breathe them out. Breathe in the fresh air. Breathe naturally.

This is an ancient Qi Gong stance of aligning the body which can trigger shifts of energy and healing. It is known as the Wu Ji posture. To come out of the posture relax your body and take a few steps around where you are standing. You can also brush your body down with your hands, shake your hands.

Come to rest, finish.

Notice how you feel, in your body. Notice how you feel in your mind. Take your time.

Accept these feelings. This is how you feel in this moment. Rest in this present moment, just as it is.

Slowly look up to the sky and raise your arms to embrace the sky. Turn your palms to face each other and imagine the sky is illuminating your whole body with healing calming light. Let your arms come down to your sides as slowly as you can. Gently gaze to the horizon once more. Do this gently and slowly three times and then rest and sense the effect.

Observe how you are feeling. If you need to do some more vigorous shaking do so and come to rest once more.

Find a place to sit down, feet on the ground, hands in your lap, head and spine sitting in dignified pose. Rest in the now.

Bring your awareness to follow your breath without changing it. In and out.

When you are ready, connect with the loving kindness and compassion in your heart. Know that it is always there, sometimes hidden, but always present to connect with.

Sooner or later the irritation can begin to dissolve away through your body and out through your fingers and toes, into the earth.

Only do this when you feel ready and do not force it. Stay in touch with, and accept without judgment, your present feelings in this present moment. Be the witness of the feelings but not the prisoner of them.

Notice your surroundings, the sights, the smells, the sounds and connect.

Notice whether you are now having any insights about what happened. Rest in non-judgment but also accept your feelings as valid and understandable. Perhaps you can also have insights and understanding about the person you argued with.

Let go of the argument. Make that your intention.

We tend to relive painful experiences and in so doing keep triggering the same pain and anger over and over, causing further suffering to ourselves. Relax your shoulders, Let go, let go, let go, for that is the path to inner freedom.

Cultivate kindness and compassion, first to yourself, then to others you had difficulty with, then to all beings. This is of huge benefit to your health and well-being.

Stay in relaxed stillness for as many minutes as you wish. End with a blessing such as:

May peace be in my heart and may I be happy and well. I wish this for all beings.

STILLNESS AND MOVEMENT

I recommend times of both sitting meditation and of Qi Gong practice which is a kind of movement meditation. This is a practice originally from China and can be traced back thousands of years. It contains both movement and gestures held in stillness as your essential subtle energy reorganises itself.

Qi means life force energy and *Gong* means to cultivate. This along with Tai Chi is what you see many Chinese people practising in parks every day as essential health and well-being practice. The slow movements are geared to longevity and fitness, a balanced mind and body, and creativity. This practice sees the mind and the spirit as equally important as the body in maintaining a healthy life.

QI GONG MEDITATION

To connect with your Qi (life force energy. Qi is pronounced 'chee')

You can either sit or stand to do this exercise with feet parallel about hip width apart.

Rub the palms of your hands together vigorously for ten seconds.

Hold your arms out in front of you with your palms facing each other about two feet apart.

Imagine there is a bar of pure energy connecting your palms.

If you push your palms very gently and subtly towards each other, you may feel a resistance.

Explore this Qi field between your palms as if your hands are connected by the energy between them. You may feel warm or hot after a couple of minutes. You may begin to feel an 'effortless effort' of holding your arms out. You may not and that is OK.

Now allow your hands to slowly return to your sides or to your lap.

This is an exploratory exercise in feeling the Qi, the energy field that is in and around all of us and all phenomena. This Qi energy can be cultivated, refined and strengthened, in many forms to give better health, longer life, more creativity.

BECOME THE WATCHER

Come home to yourself, watching yourself and life just as it is.

You can choose to be this way at any time, whatever you are doing.

You can sit in silence and stillness.

WATCH YOUR BREATH

Watch your breath coming in and going out without changing it or judging it. See this as your place of safety and of inspiration. You can adopt this method whatever you may be doing, but also seated in your meditation place, silent and still.

FOLLOW A MANTRA

Mantra literally means a *tool for the mind.* Silently recite or sing a secret or shared repetitive prayer over and over. The power of repetition is great and can overcome negative thoughts and emotions.

You can practice this with the mantra AHAM PREMA

Aham Prema is a mantra to engender love within. This is an ancient language called Sanskrit and means I AM LOVE. Traditionally, we chant a mantra multiple times to fully embed the vibration.

OM

Even simpler would be to chant OM.

This is a very ancient Vedic syllable dating back to 1,200BC and representing the primordial sound of the universe. It also reminds us that everything has a beginning, a middle, and an end.

Take a breath and make an *orrrr* sound, gradually closing your lips to an *mmmm* sound at the end of the breath... then breathe in and repeat for as many times as you wish.

It is fine if it is once or more. Let your voice note be what it is. It is your unique soul sound.

Sit quietly afterwards and sense the effect.

The mantra sounds are pure energy and vibration. The vibration moves through the body physically and spiritually bringing more harmony and positive energy to your body and mind.

One of the most well-known chants is:

OM MANI PADME HUM

The syllables mean:

Om represents the universe,

ma purifies jealousy,

ni purifies passion and desire,

pad purifies ignorance and prejudice,

me purifies poverty and possessiveness,

hum purifies aggression and hatred.

It is often translated as 'The jewel is in the lotus.' The mud which you, the lotus flower, needs to grow and bloom, can be cleaned to reveal the jewel of pure love inside you. The mud of life is necessary for beauty and wisdom to emerge.

The classic ways to chant are to be seated and close your eyes. Begin to chant the syllables. The number of times traditionally practised is 108. This number ensures the vibrations of the chant are well established within you and touch all the energy points identified in ancient healing systems. You may count with mantra beads or an abacus, or just for a period of time. One hundred and eight chants take approximately thirty minutes to complete.

However, you may chant your mantra twenty-seven times, nine times, or even less and still benefit.

EXPERIMENT WITH THE FOUR STAGES OF RECITING A CHANT:

Let us choose the chant OM NAMAH SHIVAYA for this practice. This chant is thousands of years old and means *Salutations to Shiva,* but the best secular definition I have come across is 'Salutations to all that I am capable of becoming.' Do not get too concerned with meaning but concentrate on the effect.

The four stages of chanting are:

1. To speak the syllables over and over, for a minute or so,
2. Then to whisper the syllables, over and over, for a minute or so,
3. Then to chant them in your mind silently, over and over, for a minute or so,
4. Finally, to stop and be silent. Close your eyes, and bring your awareness to your Third Eye, a point on your forehead between the eyes and slightly above them.

Rest and sense the effect. You may find golden light radiating upwards through the crown of your head, but just be as you may be. When you are ready gently open your eyes, keeping them soft.

Make sure you ground yourself afterwards by becoming aware of your physical body and your feet on the ground before leaving.

There is research to show the benefits of chanting to our health and well-being. The sound vibrations can be felt for some time after throughout the body, so be kind to yourself.

HONG SAU MEDITATION

You may choose to try the Hong Sau meditation, which was advocated by the guru Paramahansa Yogananda, and means I am Spirit. The practice can assist the development of peace, calm and vital energy.

Begin by breathing in for the mental count of six... holding it for six... and breathing out for six. Do this a few times and you should feel calmer.

Close your eyes and bring your internal gaze the point of the Third Eye, between your brows, so a slightly upward gaze. Return to a forward internal gaze if you find any discomfort.

With closed eyes begin mentally to chant Hong on the in breath and Sau (pronounced 'Saw') on the out breath. Keep your breath perfectly natural and continue for as many minutes as you can without stress or force. Yogananda told us that the longer you do this the more peaceful, calm, and kind you will become. Try it for ten minutes and increase the time in subsequent meditations if you wish.

Hong Sau is the practice of the breath and is a helpful anchor to follow your breath in meditation.

BODY AND MIND SCAN

To still the body and calm the mind.

Place your awareness at your feet and relax the soles, heels, toes, and tops of the feet. Relax your ankles. Now the back and front of the legs. Relax your knees and the backs of the knees. Travelling in your awareness up the thighs and resting at the hips, allow any tension in your legs to dissolve and run out of the legs, through the feet and out through the toes into the earth.

Become aware of your buttocks and the base of your spine and feel free to adjust your position to be as comfortable as possible. Relax your belly and your spine maintaining an upright posture, alert yet relaxed.

Bring your awareness to the heart area and imagine softening your heart. Breathe clear pure air into your lungs and exhale like a sigh.

Soften your shoulders and let them relax.

Adjust your head to a natural and comfortable position on top of the neck.

Now relax the roots of your hair and come to the face. Let the muscles around your eyes go soft, as well as the muscles around your jawline.

Allow your arms to be extremely relaxed with hands resting in your lap.

With eyes closed we rest here as the body is stilled and relaxed, all tension melts away.

Now we come to the mind and begin to allow thoughts and feelings to arise and pass naturally.

IMAGINE YOU ARE A PEBBLE IN THE STREAM

This is one of the simplest ways to meditate as described by Thich Nhat Hanh. Sit in your meditation posture. Imagine you are a pebble thrown into a stream. You slowly glide down through the water and come to rest on the bed of the stream. Stay and breathe naturally, the in breath, the out breath. Stay for as long as needed.

Truly rest and let go.

If you wish to recite a mantra, try saying to yourself a few times,

'I am calm, I am still, I am happy.'

As thoughts arise let them go on without becoming attached them, like leaves floating past in the stream

KATH READE

CHAPTER FIVE

GUIDED MEDITATIONS FOR YOUR PRACTICE

FIFTEEN MINUTE BASIC GUIDED MEDITATION

Meditation can feel daunting if we suspect that we are afraid to stay with our own feelings Well, the solution is to stay, stay, stay. It can be like going through a pain barrier. We will discover that we can stay with our feelings. We will discover that they do not stay the same, and we can watch them come, change, and go. As we stay for the show in meditation, all kinds of experiences can show up. Pleasant, unpleasant, and neutral. We stay for it all. Sometimes our back hurts, and while we can move a little to relieve it, we continue to stay with whatever arises. Sometimes visions of beauty play before our eyes, all is possible.

Just be with it, coming back to your breath as your anchor. Wherever your mind wanders, you can always come back to your breath.

Now, get as comfortable as you can and have loving kindness towards your body, especially where there are aches and pains, bring loving kindness to them. Sit on a chair, or on the floor in an upright position, hands in your lap or resting on your thighs, and close your eyes.

Bring your awareness to your breath. Leave it natural, do not change it. Keep coming back to that as many times as needed, that is the practice.

Stay sitting quietly with your eyes closed for fifteen minutes...

When it is time to come out of the meditation. When you are ready, open your eyes with a gentle downward gaze, and you can stretch.

You can finish with a blessing, here is the one I say:

May all beings live in peace.

May all beings live in harmony.

May all beings live in peace and harmony.

Do be kind and gentle with yourself for the rest of the day, and keep this kind of coming home to yourself, being with your true self, who you really are. Just keep in that space for a while in your heart and try to have nothing but love for yourself and other beings.

Fifteen Minutes Daily Meditation – Follow The Breath

Welcome to this meditation. You are very welcome for our fifteen-minute daily meditation.

A daily meditation practice can be like a daily cleansing to your body, heart, and mind.

So that is what we are about really with these daily meditations, establishing regular daily practice and seeing how that works on a cumulative basis. We can consider a few words of preparation to get us into the meditation and then share together this precious silence and stillness.

Find a posture on your chair or cushion where you can sit erect without being rigid, and let your body be firmly planted on the earth, connected to the earth.

Your hands resting easily, your heart soft, and your eyes closed gently.

Feel your body, and consciously soften any obvious tensions.

Let go of habitual thoughts and plans, bring your attention to feel the sensations of breathing.

Can you feel coolness as the air enters your nose or throat? Feel the movement of the chest, the rise of the belly. Now, take a few deeper breaths, in through the nose, out through the mouth, just breathe in, and out. Let the shoulders go down a few notches as you breathe out. Then breathe in … and out. Breathe in … breathe out.

Just get comfortable, adjust your posture if you need to at this point, and now let your breath become completely natural. Relax into each breath as you feel it, without needing to change it. Notice the soft sensations of breathing, coming, and going, and after a while your mind may wander. When you notice this, just gently come back to the breath, and softly give a word to yourself for where you have been, for example, thinking, planning, itching … and gently return to feel the next breath.

It does not matter how many times you do this; this is the practice. So, all things arise, all things pass, there is a letting go. Just sitting together in silence, following the breath.

(Silence for 15 minutes' meditation)

After fifteen minutes it is time to begin to come out of this meditation. With a gentle downward gaze, open your eyes, and keep them soft. Come back to the physical feeling of your body touching the ground in order to become grounded.

Every meditation is different so stick with it and, ideally, build up to thirty minutes a day, forty-five minutes a day. However even a few minutes a day can be beneficial. When Mahatma Gandhi was asked what he did if he was too busy to meditate every morning as was his practice, he answered that he would get up earlier.

When we meditate, we enter our own beautiful inner temple. We find all things arise from sadness and anger, frustration and grief, to happiness and a sense of freedom.

Fifteen Minutes Meditation - Finding Personal Sovereignty

So, just get comfortable in a meditation position, and just take some time to really feel that you are comfortable. This is not about sadism or anything like that. So just become restful and let your shoulders go down. You can close your eyes if you wish.

I am going to speak for a few minutes and then we will have a few minutes of silence. So, as you sit in your meditation pose, just let the words that I speak wash over you.

Generally, we are looking to arrive at a state of balance in our relationships, where each person in the relationship has their own agency, their own power, their own sovereignty.

I can remember when I was a social worker, long ago in Manchester, and a group of neighbours contacted social services about an old man who was living alone in squalor and chaos, and they said he really needed to be put into care, into an old people's home. So, I was dispatched to go and see him, but when I got there, he was perfectly compos mentis and said, 'I don't want to go into care, I want to stay here, and that's my right, isn't it?'

I said 'Yes, it is.'

One of the code of ethics principles that we were taught was a person's right to self-determination, and I have always remembered the importance of someone having the right to determine their own way forward, even if it seems, to us, to be crazy and ill-judged. We can perhaps make our feelings known with kindness, but they have the right to be on their journey. It is a form of love to acknowledge another's freedom. Of course, when a person is down, we see that and then we can walk beside them in the darkness, until they can see their own light again.

Sometimes we realise that we are so worried all the time about other people, we do not have time to be happy. Meditation, in the midst of these dilemmas, can bring so much wisdom and peace. There is a lot to be said for giving yourself that space, putting down your worries for fifteen minutes a day.

There is a Buddhist story of the Happy Monk who had once been a king. He was very wealthy, very powerful. But he was extremely worried and stressed. He was attached to wealth and power and responsibilities for his subjects. He became a monk, sitting alone in the forest. He no longer had a need for an armed guard, and his meditations led him to a greater inner peace, greater than he had ever known.

He was so happy in that forest with nothing but his robe and his bowl. We can examine our attachments with a fresh eye when we consider this story and ask ourselves what we really need, and what we can let go of.

We can release those we love, to fully empower them in their lives, but we can be here for them. We can acknowledge that they have their own wings, and they must learn to fly their own sky. We can rejoice in their independence and, in so doing, regain a sense of our own freedom, our own light. All these insights can come to us like blessings through meditation. We meditate for wisdom, for inner peace and all around us will benefit.

The spiritual teacher Ram Dass is said to have commented that if you think you are enlightened, then go and spend a week with your family. If you have a problem in your family, I encourage you to come to the meditation seat, come to the present moment, to bring you some relief, some breathing space, and some greater insight to support you.

And so let us sit together for fifteen minutes in silence. Let the following words percolate through us by repeating them silently, 'May we be filled with loving kindness.'

DIDGERIDOO SOUND JOURNEY MEDITATION

So, today we are going to listen to a meditation which I composed along with Rob Van Santé, my recording engineer and wonderful musician. Together we formed a duo called 'Deepsong' and made a CD which is called 'Dream Awake'. It has two tracks on it, a drum meditation journey, and a didgeridoo meditation journey. You can download the tracks from iTunes or choose any fifteen to twenty-minute didgeridoo track on YouTube.

Today we are going to meditate to the Deepsong didgeridoo sound journey. Just to make sure you know; it is best not to listen to this while driving or operating machinery. It is called 'The Mantra of Existence' and you will hear me speaking, playing the guitar, and singing as well as the didgeridoo. You might want to use headphones for a truer sound, so sit or lie in a comfortable position. If sitting, have your back straight, your eyes closed and breathe naturally in and out. Take a deeper breath to begin, in through your nose and out through your mouth. Just with your natural breathing, let these sounds simply be, without you intervening in any way, just be and allow. Listeners often have a blissful and relaxing experience, leaving them nourished and with deeply replenished life force energy.

Just to set the scene, here is what is said to be a 40,000-year-old Aboriginal prayer,

> May the fire be in our eyes and ears.
>
> We pray that we may hear with a deep, deep listening.
>
> So that we may hear the flow of water.
>
> And of all creation.
>
> And the dreaming.
>
> And may the fire be in our whole being.
>
> In our legs and feet.
>
> Enabling us to walk the earth with reverence and care.

So that we may walk in the ways of goodness and truth.

And may the fire be in our eyes may open our eyes to share what is good in life.

That is the challenge to us. How much deeper can we go to really get the richness from solitude and from opportunities to meditate and really think deeper into our soul for greater and greater insights and inner wisdom, ultimately, peace?

We can simply rest and meditate to the playing of the didgeridoo and benefit from the repetitive vibrations which will harmonise our own energy centres. It is traditional to light some sage to 'smudge' which is to purify the air of any negativity. We are not sitting around a campfire, but we do have the fires of lighting a candle for our inner flame if desired. May we have a beautiful sound journey together.

Didgeridoo Sound Journey

I am the earth

I am the tree.

I am the fire

I am the sea

I am the snake

I am the bear

I am freedom

I am the air

I walk my footsteps

Across the sand

I walk my footsteps

Across the land.

I feel the wind

Across my face

Mother Earth is our sacred space

(Words by Kath Reade)

After the didgeridoo has finished, I encourage you to sit in silence now for as long as you wish and just sense the effect. Just breathing naturally and just as if we are sitting around a fire by the sea, on the sand. We hear the waves gently coming in on the in-breath, and our out- breath is when the wave gently recedes and goes out. Just have that in mind as you sit in beautiful silence, and sense the effect of the sound vibrations.

(Several minutes' silent meditation)

So, we begin to come out of this meditation. Open your eyes when you are ready with a gentle downward gaze.

We finish with a blessing:

May all beings live in peace.

May all beings live in harmony.

May all beings live in peace and harmony.

The didgeridoo meditation and a Shamanic drumming journey is on the CD 'Dream awake' by Deepsong available from www.kathreade.co.uk and downloadable on iTunes.

I am sending blessings to you and hoping that you can use these meditations to help you manage whatever may be going on for you in your life.

There is a saying which originated in Christianity, which encourages us to change the things we can change, to accept the things that we cannot change, and have the wisdom to know the difference. Silent meditation will help us to embody this wisdom, and sound vibrations will embody this wisdom deep within us at a molecular level.

A DAILY INTENTION FOR SELF CARE GUIDED MEDITATION

I want to share with you a daily intention for self-care, which I wrote a while back and I have been practising with. Because after my life experience of looking after my mother who was very seriously ill for many years when I was young, and then going straight into social work in Manchester, followed by community activism and leading NHS boards, I never really put myself first. In fact, in many ways, I neglected myself.

I thought self-care meant selfishness, and after much personal development work, now I know it does not, so I would like to share this with you. A daily intention for self-care. It is something I am slowly learning to do much better now, and I wish that for you. I recommend that you read this aloud to yourself regularly and then sit quietly and sense the effect. Sit in your favourite spot for meditation, comfortably and recite this intention for yourself with a sense of kindness in your heart.

MY DAILY INTENTION FOR SELF CARE

I am loving my body.

Into the highest health and harmony.

To my pain, I bring love.

To my discomfort, I bring balm.

To my harsh thoughts, I bring kindness.

Where disease may gather, I dissolve all blockages in my life force energy.

With flowing compassion, I release deeply held trauma and all negativity.

I fill my body and spirit, heart and mind with loving kindness and peace.

My fervent vow, before the altar of my soul fire,

Is to accord love to myself which is equal to the love I bestow upon others.

I become my own best friend, and I know this is coming to pass in this very moment.

I seal this intention with a kiss on my hand and a hug for myself.

In the sure knowledge that I take the right action at the right time for my highest good.

And so, for the good of others.

And so shall it be, in the name of all life and love.

From the butterfly wing to the mountain.

From the skylark to the deep ocean.

Now close your eyes and let these words simply percolate through your being without effort. Try to relax your body and mind with kindness.

I have made it a practice to say this self-compassion prayer, regularly, and I offer it to you. If you want to make it your practice too, I would be very honoured. Over time the practice will become part of who you are.

Blessings.

Loving Kindness Guided Meditation

I invite you to a short loving kindness meditation. If you wish to take up a meditation posture you are familiar with, then take up your own posture. Otherwise take a comfortable seat and sit in a position which is relaxed, yet quite erect. Become aware of your feet, connecting with Mother Earth and imagine your head with a golden cord connecting you to the cosmic energy source life force. Then you can just clasp your hands in your lap to close your eyes if you want.

The practice of loving kindness is a very ancient one. It is really a gift to yourself to cultivate your loving kindness, compassion, forgiveness and with this comes, in time, a measure of inner peace. We come to the present moment. The past is gone, the future is not here yet, and all we have, all we ever have, is this present moment. So, let us just inhabit that for a moment, sit together and just arrive here. Become aware of your breath, breathing in, and breathing out. Now let it be as relaxed as possible. You do not have to change it, just follow it by being aware of your breath as your anchor.

You may have heard the old story about the Native American Indian grandfather talking with his grandson. He says to him, "You, and everyone, were born with two hungry wolves inside you. One of your hungry wolves is always angry, jealous, resentful, and mean, and the other hungry wolf inside you is loving, generous, kind, compassionate, joyful, and happy. Whichever wolf you feed the most is the wolf that will grow the biggest."

This story is the gist of this short meditation because if we take up the practice of loving kindness in this spirit, then we are cultivating within ourselves the seeds of compassion and kindness, and that applies equally towards ourselves as well as to others.

So, we can begin with ourselves as we say,

May I be filled with loving kindness.

May I be well and happy.

May I live in peace and with ease.

Continue to repeat these words either out loud or inside your head, two or three times

May I be filled with loving kindness.

May I be well and happy.

May I live in peace and with ease.

Sit in silence and sense the effect.

Next, we extend these wishes to somebody else that we love, and that we think about, someone we wish well, and so we say,

May you be filled with loving kindness

May you be well and happy

May you live in peace and with ease

Again, after two or three times, sit in silence for a couple of minutes and let this infuse through your being, and sense the effect.

Now we think of someone we find difficult and try to imagine the sorrow in their lives that has led to their dissatisfaction. We wish them well and know this is very good for our own health. We say,

May they be filled with loving kindness

May they be well and happy

May they live in peace and with ease

Take three deeper breaths, breathing out toxins in your system with each out-breath, and sense the effect.

Then we extend our loving kindness practice to all beings, and we say this time,

May all beings be filled with loving kindness.

May all beings be well and happy.

May all beings live in peace and with ease.

Then we come back to the beginning, to ourselves.

When you feel the time is right, sit for a few minutes in silence.

We end the meditation by returning to our first loving kindness mantra,

May I be filled with loving kindness

May I be well and happy

May I live in peace and with ease.

Now, let your whole body relax, soften your eyes, and your belly, and your heart. Sit for a few more minutes following the breath, before opening your eyes, keeping them soft. If you have any bells like the Tingsha bells or a Tibetan singing bowl you can ring them to signify the end of the meditation.

So, I encourage you to honour your feelings. All of us have the wolf of anger and hurt, betrayal, jealousy, resentment, alongside our wolf of loving kindness and generosity. Honour it all, but at the same time we practise loving kindness because we believe in the better part of ourselves. It can be done, we can go a long way to cultivate loving kindness towards ourselves and others. The benefits to your own well-being can be immense. Namaste. (This is a Sanskrit blessing pronounced na-mast-ay, and means 'The spirit in me honours the spirit in you')

A traditional way to complete your meditation is to put your palms together at your heart, with thumbs at your sternum, bow your head, and say Namaste, especially if you are with others.

CHAPTER SIX

MEDITATION READINGS

Readings are helpful to open or close the meditation session.

STAYING WITH THE ART OF LOVE

What can we do in the face of this world of seeming chaos?

Your face is sad, your heart is heavy.

We can stay with the heart of peace.

We stay with the art of love.

We will send the energy of our peaceful hearts up into the ether, filling the air,

the earth, the sea, and our hunger for peace and justice will spread.

Being the peace we want to see is a strong way to be.

Founded on meditation practice.

Sending the energy of peace, love, justice, and reconciliation across the world.

We already know the root of anger is hurt, lack of love.

Lack of longevity, injustice, violence, deprivation, abandonment.

Can we understand these roots of violence?

One day this will be understood and acted upon...

without the empty kneejerk reaction of more violence and war.

This will be when the majority speak out with the longing for peace in their hearts.

For now, we fill the ether with universal love for all beings.

Simply take your meditation seat and breathe.

Take a deep breath in and breathe out slowly.

You can make your intention to let go of the negativity of your fear and despair.

Simply, breathe the breath of peace and love. Do not let it be extinguished.

Keep the flower of peace and love blooming in your heart,

for your sake, for the world's sake.

THE TRUTH THAT LIVES INSIDE YOU

So many people try to sell you answers to your life.
The true answer costs nothing but your time.
Time to listen deeply to your own inner voice.
Give time to be in that stillness within.
Go below the noise of anxiety, stress, worry,
the harsh judgments of the self-punisher.
Go beyond those clammering voices,
seek the still calm voice beneath,
the epiphany of your truth.
Hear that for it is never wrong.
It is the authentic voice of self-care, at last.
May you always be kind to yourself
May you live in love.

FORGIVENESS, FOR YOUR SAKE

Cultivate forgiveness as your essential healthcare.

Every time you remember the hurt, it has the power to hurt you again.

Forgive more. Forgive others and yourself instantly.

I forgive you. I forgive me. Instantly.

Why not?

Recite the Ho'oponopono as though your life depends on it, for it does.

I'm sorry, please forgive me, thank you. I love you.

This will prevent emotional congestion in the heart, liver, and lungs.

Meditate and dance slowly to Indian raga music every day, calm and creative.

Nourish the powerhouse of your meditation.

Let go of negativity. Let the sun shine inside and smile.

Let go of that which no longer serves you, with effortless effort.

Bless you

Namaste

(N.B. The Ho'oponopono is the traditional Hawaiian practice of forgiveness.)

MEDITATION OF THE SEVEN VEILS

May my meditation today be like
The Dance of the Seven Veils.
With each layer that I let go, let go, let go,
there is a deeper revelation, naked truth,
and greater inner freedom.
I untie the veil of fear, of aversion, of not wanting,
And let it go.
I untie the veil of grasping, of desire, of wanting,
And let it go.
I untie the veil of illusions, endless illusions,
And let it go.
I untie the veil of judgment, good and bad,
And let it go.
I untie the veil of the past, for it is gone,
And let it go.
I untie the veil of the future, not here yet,
And let it go.
I untie the veil of ego, the 'I' of 'I am',
And let it go.
I take the one seat,
Allowing compassion and kindness
To shine endlessly
In a heart of joy and peace.
I watch the sky, and all is revealed.

REFUGE COMES WITH SILENCE

Refuge comes with silence,
Silence is a gift.
To still the mind, I watch my thoughts,
Like white horses over darkest blue, ever arising.
My true spirit is not the waves so much as the deep ocean.
I am not the clouds, but the infinite sky.

My body revels in sanctuary, I love every cell.
I bring my loving kindness to my pain and stress.
I imagine the loving hands, of a kind being
Caressing away my discomfort.
My eyes are soft with love.
My body relaxes with a long sigh of relief
I am home.
At last, my compassion includes myself.
I rest calmly amid the noise and tumult.
I cannot quiet the world, but I can become quiet,
Accepting what is, in this moment, and this moment.
Dwelling in the now,
Detached and caring at the same time is my salvation.
Now I see, joy is completely possible, and beckons.
I glide like an eagle over this world of pain and beauty
I have perspective, I have empathy, I survive,
Through the grace of calm meditation
I weather the storms,

I breathe and walk,
Dance and sing,
Laugh and love.

CALM SPIRIT COME

Calm spirit come to our hearts and minds.

Pour the loving oil of calm and compassionate care on our wounds,

on our thwarted desires, our anger, our disaffection, our cravings,

our petty vanities and our irritations,

our many delusions and avoidances of what we find unable to face.

Let it all simply melt and evaporate like sea spray on a sun-warmed rock.

All things must change, all things shall pass.

Let us truly be in the flow of our life's journey,

trusting in both our patience and wise action as our way forward.

Cultivating compassion, and a constantly loving heart in our stillness and silence.

In this way we build capacity, resilience, to weather the storms.

Being in the flow, letting go, knowing the water goes on flowing

with or without us, enjoying the ride.

Knowing the tranquillity of infinity, remembering our courage,

using our ingenuity, rooted in our love and compassion for ourselves, and for others.

We are mostly made of water,

water within, water without, go with the flow,

in the symphony of vibration that is our body, mind, and heart, and all things.

The parts of our soul that broke away with every painful trauma

can now be brought back and reunited,

resonating with that vibrant energy which is pre-natal and which goes on forever.

We flow from form to form.

Hear the deep song of your pure golden being, and the music of your true spirit.

REST RESTORE AND REACH FOR YOUR DREAMS

Rest, restore, and reach for your dreams

Happiness is an art. It is not a state,

for that is too vulnerable to the whims of ever-changing circumstance.

Happiness can be cultivated, tended, watered, shone upon, and loved.

Then shall the techniques and the art of cultivating happiness produce a resilient happiness,

akin to the sensations of a joy that has no reason to be joyful. It just is.

It will not be weak and short-lived like a forced hot house plant,

but tenacious and enduring like the olive tree planted in Roman times, still flourishing today.

Happiness is an art that can be practised.

Become the gardener of your joy, an evergreen that cannot be quelled.

CLOSING BLESSING

(Light a candle)

WHILE I AM IN THE LIGHT LET ME ADORE IT

While I am in the light let me adore it
And while I am in the darkness let this candle signify my flame
Let the toxins within flow out until my heart is pure love.
Let darker thoughts fly out from my mind
Let my body feel lighter
as the lava of trauma slowly moves on and out.
    I allow it.
Let me be with the ebb and flow of my earthly existence,
keeping my soul-eyes on the candle flame of hope for a better day,
which will surely come, for all is impermanent.
With meditation as my rock and inspiration,
I will keep my candle burning
at the window of my life,
And pray for all beings.
May all beings know happiness.
May all beings live in peace and harmony.

CHAPTER SEVEN

COMMUNITY MEDITATION AS PUBLIC SERVICE

HOW TO HOLD A MEDITATION GROUP

There are neighbourhoods and communities who have not had the opportunity to practice or explore meditation because it has not been present in their history or sub-culture.

In areas where there are relatively high levels of poor health, isolation, loneliness, and low income, there is often a correlation with high crime and low educational attainment. In these communities we see high levels of anxiety and depression, drug and alcohol use, and low expectations.

Statistics show that life expectancy in such areas of Britain are generally ten years less on average.

We are in difficult times. Many people are stressed. I personally turned to meditation at my lowest in 1998 after a period of very high stress and found it to be a lifesaver.

OFFERING A MEDITATION GROUP

If you wish to be of service to your own community, you can offer a meditation group session with the emphasis on sharing quiet time together to let go of stress and cultivate relaxation and peace of mind.

You can hold a weekly or fortnightly group meditation for an hour and advertise it locally and on social media and/or invite people you know may be interested.

You will need to find a suitable room to meet that has chairs and ventilation and can be a relatively quiet place. Ideally you can use this room for free or a small hire charge. These rooms can be in sought in community centres, libraries, yoga centres or similar.

If there is a table in the room you may want to bring some flowers or a small buddha, or some meditation bells (Tingsha Bells) to create a conducive space.

It is important to decide the maximum number this room can comfortably hold and decide on your covid awareness measures. E.g., distance between people, provision of hand sanitiser etc. You may find the organisation has requirements for the use of the room in this regard. Usually the average number of chairs would be ten, arranged in a circle.

It is helpful to be adaptable and flexible, and to be a deeply sensitive and intuitive listener to people from all walks of life and backgrounds. We suspend judgments and offer a place people can come and be accepted as themselves.

Our aim is to encourage and support anyone to participate in meditation so that they too can cultivate a sense of inner peace and joy. So that they too can strengthen their emotional resilience to carry them through the storms and deprivations of life.

The underlying principle and offer is kindness and non-judgment.

Anyone, from whatever background or circumstance, can be offered the immense benefits of a regular meditation practice.

We can spell out in the invitation to the session that the benefits of meditation include:

More relaxation

Better health and well being

More inner peace

Better sleep

Joy in simple pleasures

Blood pressure may lower

More emotional resilience to deal with problems

More creativity

More happiness, better mood

You need to decide if you want an open-door policy to attend any or all sessions, or whether you prefer people to sign up for a course of six or more sessions. I have found the open-door policy tends to attract more attendees, but attendance can be more variable.

It is very important to discover who the opinion formers and influencers are informally. Try to be alive to how the centre users are thinking and get to know people. You will become aware of issues that could help you to pitch your session and attract potential participants. There are usually all sorts of personalities and alliances at play.

Try to get the organisation that is hiring the room to you to advertise your meditation group on their website and on their noticeboards. You can make a poster or even have flyers printed to invite people and ask local shops, supermarkets, libraries to put them in their windows. It is a good idea to contact your local newspaper and radio station to see if they will give some coverage and maybe interview you.

You may want to use a digital booking system with a maximum number of places. You can create an event on Facebook to advertise this with a link to book. These sites do most of the admin work for you and you are notified by e mail when someone has booked a place (e.g., Eventbrite.com or Bookwhen.com etc.) There is usually an administration fee.

It is useful to give some thought to the health challenges some people may have in attending. Seek a fully accessible building with a disabled toilet where possible.

It does not have to be all about following the breath if you have a meditation group in an area with poor health and high rates of respiratory illness. In that case you can offer participants who have breathing problems the option to bring their awareness back to their feet as their anchor in the meditation rather than struggle with following their breath.

These measures are so that the benefits of meditation can be offered to people who have not meditated nor seen themselves as meditators. This is the challenge. The results are worth the effort.

Here you will find insights and guidelines which can be useful to anyone wishing to hold a meditation with others. These were gleaned from my weekly meditations in a community centre in a very deprived area of Burnley.

POINTS TO REMEMBER:

Qualification and Training

At the time of writing there is no requirement to have a qualification to teach meditation, but it is advisable to learn as much as you can about the practice of meditation, and I would recommend you find a meditation teacher to teach you.

It would also be beneficial to be trained in basic first aid in case of medical emergency or have someone in your meditation group or in the building who is a first-aider.

You may want to compile a list of helping organisations to have an idea of how to refer people on to specific help such as mental health that you may not be qualified to advise on.

Code of Ethics

The relationship between you and the attendees of a meditation group needs to be bound by a code of ethics equivalent to a teacher and students. This code usually includes a general policy statement such as this:

'We believe everyone should be treated equally regardless of race, sex, gender identification, sexual orientation, national origin, native language, religion, age, disability, marital status, citizenship, genetic information, pregnancy, or any other characteristic protected by law.' (AIHR Academy to Innovate HR)

Other principles should be included such as respecting confidentiality and the right of students to self-determination. The facilitator should never be inappropriate in their behaviour but should be always professional and courteous.

Insurance Cover

It would be wise to arrange insurance cover to teach meditation and there are companies who offer cover for meditation, mindfulness, and alternative therapies. You need cover for any adverse events.

Disclaimer

Medical disclaimers are a short form of legal words which let people know you are not going to give medical advice, that you do not accept liability for people's medical issues, and people should continue to follow their medics advice and treatment. This can be printed on your website, for example.

Organisational points

Arrange the room beforehand with chairs in a circle.

Stick to a regular meeting time and place.

Advertise – be clear about charge or no charge. The tradition is not for profit, so an optional or nominal donation to cover room hire, advertising and refreshments would be usual.

Always start and finish on time or people will come late and leave early.

Always give time for the participants to become physically grounded again before they leave.

You may ask if anyone wants to say anything and give time for this. It is about listening to them rather than judging what they say. Sometimes we can suggest that there are a few moments of quiet after a person has spoken to give time for their words to be fully acknowledged.

Decide on music or no music. This can vary from session to session. You may concentrate on silence or sound, stillness or gentle meditational movements and alternate these modalities in your sessions.

Start your sessions with the emphasis on the gift of silence. You may want to incorporate soothing sounds. You can learn the benefits of chanting and how to incorporate chanting and/or sound healing music into your meditation session. However, silence is the bedrock and is certainly enough.

HOW TO FACILITATE THE MEDITATION GROUP SESSION

Here are two examples of how you may want to run the session:

MEDITATION LEADER SCRIPT 1

To begin the session:

Welcome and invite them to sit down on a chair in a circle with others and get comfortable. Ask them to sit upright with both feet on the floor. Hands can rest in the lap. Help anyone with disabilities to find their ideal meditation position.

Briefly explain the benefits of meditation as above.

Ask the group to come to stillness and to stay still except to relieve any pain or discomfort. Then explain as follows:

Close or half close your eyes.

Stay quiet. Watch your thoughts but do not get caught up with them. Many people feel they cannot meditate because they cannot control their thoughts. Therefore, it is important to spend time talking about how to deal with thoughts. The idea is not to stop thinking but just to start noticing that you are having thoughts, this is the first step. Notice how your thoughts arise, stay, and fade. That is the practice. We try not to judge but just notice.

When you find your mind wandering, come back to awareness of your feet on the ground. Do this as many times as needed. That is the process.

Feel kindness towards yourself. Try not to criticise yourself.

Let go. Allow yourself to relax your body bit by bit from the toes to the roots of your hair.

The power is in the process of staying quiet and still for regular periods of time and a change will come over you. A growing greater tranquillity, and appreciation of the present moment, unspoiled by fears of a future that has not yet happened. Unspoiled by a past that has gone and we can do little to change.

So we rest here in the present moment and fully savour it just as it is.

To start with you can hold the space of silence for ten minutes a couple of times or more and then build to twenty minutes. The group will build their capacity to meditate for longer as you gently encourage and facilitate with kindness.

MEDITATION LEADER SCRIPT 2

WELCOME the participants. Ensure they have a seat around the circle.

EXPLAIN WHAT TO EXPECT

Meditation is the practice of stopping doing things for a while and being still and quiet, resting in the present moment. This practice can relax and re-energise us. It can calm us and bring some inner peace and joy.

Rather than looking externally for what we need, we look inward and see that if we put everything down, let go, we will find that inner peace and joy inside of ourselves. Do not force this but let it happen in its own time by simply allowing and letting go.

ADVICE ON POSTURE

Sit upright on your chair with your feet connecting to the ground. Close your eyes and rest your hands in your lap. Devote some time to getting as comfortable as possible so you can be still for a while

RELAX THE BODY

Try to feel where you are holding tension in your body and relax. Let it go. Let it go. Let go.

Go slowly through the Body Scan to still the body. (See Body Scan Meditation)

Silent Pause …………

CALM THE MIND

Mind awareness. Encourage the participants to let thoughts of the past and future go. Just watch thoughts arise and drift away without getting involved in them. Like watching clouds across a windy sky.

Silent Pause ....

FOLLOW YOUR BREATH

Come to the awareness of your breath. Your in- breath and your out- breath without changing it or judging it. Follow it just as it is like a wave coming in and then out from the shore.

Count your breaths up to 20.

When your mind wanders then keep coming back to follow your breath.

Silent Pause ....

(NB. If anyone has breathing problems, asthma etc., you can advise that they may prefer to bring their awareness to rest on their feet connecting with the earth as their anchor, rather than the breath.)

SILENT MEDITATION

Then the group sits in silence and stillness for 10 minutes or 20 minutes as you judge best. You may have two or three such short meditations in the hour giving time in between.

ENDING THE MEDITATION

End the meditation gently and slowly by speaking kindly to tell them they are coming towards the end of the meditation. Ask participants to open their eyes with a gentle downward gaze to finish the meditation

Stretch if they wish.

Advise them -Feel your feet on the earth and come back to being aware of your physical body.

End with a Blessing. E.g., May all beings know peace and joy.

Optional: You may wish to ring the Tingsha bells three times softly at this point.

PARTICIPANTS CHANCE TO SPEAK

Give the group members an opportunity to say anything they may wish to say but emphasise they do not have to speak.

NEXT SESSION

Let them know when the next session will be and warmly invite them.

Some groups have a cup of tea together after the session and this can help to get to know each other and gives an opportunity to informally discuss what happened in the session.

CHAPTER EIGHT

COMMUNITY MEDITATION IN ACTION

AN EMPIRICAL CASE STUDY DURING 2022

VANGUARD COMMUNITY CENTRE MEDITATION GROUP, BURNLEY, LANCASHIRE, UK

Introduction

Vanguard Community Centre is located in the one per cent most deprived communities in England objectively defined by the UK Government Index of Multiple Deprivation. The area is disadvantaged in every domain, housing, education and skills, income, employment, crime, health, disability, and life expectancy. Members of the meditation group subjectively define their area as one of loneliness and isolation, and of a lot of poor health.

In the 1980s and 90s, I was a community worker in the area, and an elected Burnley Borough councillor for the ward, for thirteen years. I was Leader of Burnley Council for the last four of these years. I worked closely with local people at this time and together we were able to achieve the demolition of the dilapidated deck access Trafalgar flats which were diagnosed with concrete cancer. A small estate of houses with gardens and the multi-purpose Vanguard community centre were built on the site in consultation with local residents.

Trafalgar flats, built in 1968, exhibited by the 1990s, many of the features of crumbling disorder and anti-social behaviour typical of such UK public housing deck access developments of that era and we managed to get them demolished in 1994. At the time I wrote a song about this which the long-term residents still refer to.

Search Youtube: Kath Reade Trafalgar Flats.

Twenty-eight years later in 2022, I was asked to return to run a meditation group in the very community centre I had helped to get built, and I very happily reunited with some of those residents. I am enjoying communicating with them in a totally different way, now as their meditation teacher. Here follows some of our experiences in the meditation group as an exemplar of how the benefits of meditation can be brought to such communities.

EXCERPTS FROM VANGUARD COMMUNITY CENTRE MEDITATION SESSIONS 2022

VANGUARD MEDITATION SESSION 1
RECORDED DISCUSSION ON LONELINESS

We begin with a recorded transcript of a participants discussion facilitated by me as their meditation teacher, after a silent meditation. It is reproduced here with participants permission.

S: 'You spend a lot of time working hard, trying to make enough money but I had a bad stroke and I realised, money? Oh, money's nothing. It's really all about friendship and loving one another. And during the lockdown there was so much isolation, it got fifty times worse.'

M: 'Vanguard has changed my life. Because you feel like you've got someone that wants to be your friend.'

S: 'Like gathering here today, all mixing together today.'

Kath:(speaking to 'C'). How have you found the meditation C?

C: 'Well…… because I've been so stressed. It's the first time I've actually sat and relaxed. The first thing I noticed after the meditation is I've got a finger open. (Holds her hand up.) That finger hasn't been open for six months. It's been flat on my hand like these other ones. They won't open with the arthritis, but in the meditation this one has just miraculously opened. I've got a finger open!

I think that is the first time I've actually sat down and relaxed my body and stopped feeling sorry for myself (laughs). And it was something today and I don't know what it was, perhaps the sunshine, but today I got up and was determined I was coming up here to meditation.

Every day I say, I'm going up to the centre and I never get over the door, but today I was determined I was coming – part of it was because I knew you'd be here and I wanted to see you Kath, as I hadn't seen you for ages. And part of it was… if I don't get over my own front door, I'm going to get into the state of being frightened to go out. (General agreement).

I was feeling that… erm... up to last year I thought I had a lot of friends. When I went poorly in December, with the exception of Tom, not one person has been to my door, not to ask how I am, nothing. To knock to see if I needed any shopping or just to say how are you. And it made me feel, … erm…absolutely useless, worthless. And I got to the stage where my daughter was ringing me every hour to make sure I hadn't done anything stupid. This has been a big step for me coming to meditation today. And I feel my old self is still in here…'. (emotional)

Kath: 'No doubt… there's no doubt about that! You know I was talking earlier about the flame inside of us?'

C: 'Yes'

Kath: 'Well, you still have that flame I know that.'

P: 'Yes you do.'

C: 'Yes.'

S: 'By the way, I called round to see you and I posted a letter for you. If you can remember?'

C: 'Did you? Oh right.'

Tea and biscuits arrive.

C: 'When I opened my eyes from the meditation you know,
I could see this finger had opened!'

Kath: 'I think there was a healing energy in the room……
Listen, I have just realised I had my phone still on record after our song, and it has recorded everything we have just said.
Do you want me to delete it? Because I may write a book about meditation so you could become famous.' (General laughter)

C: You have already written a song about us so, fine.

M. I am going to have to have one of those pink wafers.

VANGUARD MEDITATION SESSION 2
DON'T JUST DO SOMETHING, SIT THERE!

'There is so much love in this group, you cannot fail to take it home with you'. This was said by H, community worker, at the end of this session.

We had a few minutes silence at the beginning to fully arrive.

The guided meditation began with a simple but telling demonstration of me holding up a glass of water. I explained, 'The water will never become completely still held up in my hand and my arm will become increasingly more painful the longer I hold the glass. For the water to become completely calm and still I have to put it down. So it is with your worries and stress.... put them down and let them calm and settle......let go just for now and rest. (a Buddhist teaching)

As you scan your body with your mind's eye, become aware of any pain or discomfort and bring loving kindness to it.

This goes for emotional pain and suffering, loss, and anger. Acknowledge it all with kindness towards yourself.

If you have a physical pain, beam love to it. Do not shut down and go away from it, but go towards it and embrace your pain with loving kindness. Bring that loving kindness right to the seat or root of your pain. Become mindful of that physical pain or mental suffering and bring kindness and compassion to it.'

Next, I led the group through a body scan to relax all parts of the body, bringing awareness from your toes to the roots of your hair. Relaxing the shoulders and letting any tension flow down the arms and out through the fingertips, into the earth.

'Imagining our feet are grounding us. Like the roots of a tree into the earth. Our topmost branches may be blown around by events, but we return our awareness to our feet connecting with Mother Earth and come to stillness and silence.'

Then we sat together for some moments of stillness and silence.

There was no disturbance in the room, just a very peaceful healing energy, as though they were born to it and meditation was second nature to them.

People outside the open window were chattering again but did not disturb us. I have trained the group to accept, without irritation, any extraneous noise as part of the landscape/soundscape of our lives. We are no longer irritated or put off, even by the sound of a lawn mower, or children playing. We develop a kind tolerance for all that arises, knowing that this as all also passes. All is impermanent and so we fully live in and savour every present moment.

This is a busy community centre in the heart of a deprived community, not a temple. So I have taught that we have to make our own temple within ourselves, and accept the external circumstances. Our meditation group did this splendidly and there was a nourishing peaceful ambience in this little library room.

After gently coming out of this simple meditation, and having rung the tingsha bells three times, I asked them to keep their eyes soft and their hearts open.

I asked them to continue to show great kindness to themselves. I invited them to stretch and move but for some time they stayed in a beautiful stillness.

I invited them to share anything they wished but emphasised they did not have to say anything.

M said that for the third week running she was now totally relaxed, and her two hands were just like two heavy weights.

We gave each of them a glossy picture of a monk in orange robes meditating beside a still lake with the heading:

'Don't just do something, sit there'

(Thich Nhat Hanh)

They liked this and took it home with them.

Then I explained there are many traditions of meditation, and we would sample the native American Indian practice of drumming. This shamanic practice can be found in many cultures including the Aborigines where they refer to its effects as 'Dream Awake.'

I played the Native American elmwood flute, then began a rhythmic regular shamanic drumming pattern of four beats a second which is practised to reach the dream awake meditation state. I continued for 15 minutes without speaking.

I noticed during this that drumming meditation one lady became very hot, with red cheeks, pushing her hair away from her face and perspiring.

The rest were had closed eyes and were very still. The energy of the drum was palpable, and was deeply resonant, in the note of a low C which tends to resonate with the lower half of the body and can put one in a rather dreamlike state. It is that time between being deeply asleep and fully awake.

Every member of the group said they enjoyed the drumming meditation, and I was glad no one had had an uncomfortable experience, which can happen depending on what the drum stirs up for the listener.

I was a little apprehensive about introducing these experiences into a seemingly conventional community, but they have taken to them like a duck to water. They seem open and eager to try different meditational experiences.

Emboldened by their positive reception, I introduced a pack of cards, called 'White Eagle Medicine Wheel Deck' by Wa-Na-Nee-Che (Connections Book Publishing). I asked them to blind-choose one and ponder on its possible significance to their own lives.

The lady who had been so hot during the drumming held up her card and it was 'Sweat Lodge'

Others found they had picked a particular animal. M had the Otter card which said:

'Whatever painful circumstance has swelled into your life the Otter Spirit Animal Totem teaches us to dive under trouble and watch it roll on by.

This acrobat lives her life among jagged rocks and crashing waves. Her survival tactics on treacherous coastlines are to twirl and play. Playtime is the best medicine to heal a wounded soul. What do you find fun? Otter says, do that now. Waste no time on why you shouldn't. '

This meant a huge amount to M because she had moved to Burnley with a lot of hurt and a broken heart. After being isolated she was invited to come down to the Vanguard Community Centre, and before long started running classes.

M loved the Otter and felt the playfulness of her craftwork was a mend for her pain and loneliness.

'Since coming here I have never looked back' she said.

In these meditations I am listening with my ears and with my heart to what the group members may or may not find useful, and then choosing techniques accordingly.

Meditation usually uses awareness of the breath as the anchor to come back to. Following the in breath and the out breath and coming back to it each time the mind wanders.

But I notice several of our community centre meditators have impaired breathing because of health conditions, in which case to ask them to follow their breath is only asking them to face unnecessary difficulties.

This part of Lancashire has generally quite poor health and a lot of rainy damp weather. There is a history of respiratory problems in East Lancashire dating back beyond the times of the 19th century cotton mills and mining.

I felt the need to be sensitive to local and individual circumstances to facilitate the most helpful meditations.

The last thing I want is for them to waste their precious meditation time in struggle and concluding they cannot 'do' meditation as a result.

One lady had the card 'Wisdom Keeper' which said she kept the wisdom for her family,

'I wish they'd realise that' she quipped with a smile.

C. got the Medicine Woman card - this was an elder role who had built up the tribe. This was so apt as she and I were the ones who got the community centre built a quarter of a century ago. She was the driving force who ran the original community group from the start and built the activities there.

We reminisced about how I as Leader of the Council in the 1990s had made sure that C was given a hard hat and led into a huge digger where she was shown how to smash the first blow of a wrecking ball into the horrendous Trafalgar Deck Access Flats to begin the demolition. This made way for the building of houses with small gardens and the Vanguard Community Centre.

It meant a great deal to me to return to the centre all these years later to hold these meditations and once again be of service to this community in a completely different way as their meditation teacher.

Afterwards we had cups of tea, and a birthday cake was brought in for me which was so thoughtful.

Before they left, I asked each of the people there to give one word to describe how they were feeling after the meditation. The words they chose were calm, happy, peaceful, good, lovely, relaxed, amazing.

VANGUARD MEDITATION SESSION 3
LESSON IN LETTING GO

There was a spike in in Coronavirus in the UK this week, so I brought masks and hand sanitiser, but the attendees just did not use them. I did not feel able to insist as restrictions had been officially lifted.

I led a guided meditation to encourage relaxation. I asked them to imagine they were a pebble falling gently through the water and resting on the sandy riverbed as in Thich Nhat Hanh's meditations. I encouraged them to watch their thoughts and let them go rather than being too much identified with them.

There were a lot of questions afterwards from one lady who had a very enquiring mind. After answering some of them I encouraged her to let the questions go and suggested that all answers will come as needed from silence.

Another said she had left her spiritualist church and had been looking for somewhere to go instead. She told us she had sent healing to us all throughout the meditation.

Another participant asked if there is a particular direction you should face your Buddha ornaments towards at home. There is a great deal of advice about this. Generally, Buddha statues are recommended to be facing east. However, because we are not a Buddhist group, nor any religious group, I urged a relaxed yet respectful approach to this symbol of peace and tranquillity, and to be guided by her preference.

I mentioned chanting and sang the chant OM SHREE DANVANTRE NAMAHAH. This is a chant in Sanskrit meaning to invoke health and protection from illness. Sanskrit is an ancient language which is the Indian equivalent of Latin. They loved it and wanted more.

A young woman attended who was on work experience from a social care course. Her legs were constantly moving and fidgeting. Her face looked incredibly bored, yet I got the feeling she was getting into the meditation as time went on. Eventually she stretched out as if in bed and looked amazingly chilled and still. The slow smile she gave me on the way out was beautiful, and she became encouraging to others regarding meditation.

During the silence there was a wonderfully peaceful, tranquil energy in the room which was notably healing and nourishing.

P. regularly brews up for people in the centre, and he was very keen to make tea for us all. Although no-one asked for any, he made seven mugs of tea anyway. A very sweet and helpful man.

Meditation is the art of finding peace and happiness within, using simple methods of calming. These methods and their benefits are unfolding in our group each week.

VANGUARD MEDITATION SESSION 4

ADAPTABILITY

Our meditation session of seven people coincided perfectly with a massive steam clean of the carpets in the community centre. A continuous loud noise from an industrial sized steam cleaner threatened to scupper our silence.

I used my Tuner Lite app to discover the predominant musical note of the machine. It was G, the note of the throat chakra. I improvised by telling them this and explaining the seven chakra energy centres and their meaning.

We then tuned in with the carpet cleaner to nourish our throat chakra energy.

I told them the meaning of the OM and we sang the OM to the machine noise.

The OM exemplifies that everything has a beginning, a middle, and an end and is described as the seed sound of the universe.

The group sat quietly, and I began to sing harmonising notes around the vacuum note. It began to sound like sacred music in a church with the vacuum as the deeper continuous drone, almost reminiscent of a church organ.

As the machine gradually subsided, we sat in welcome silence for a few minutes.

One member said she had not heard the noise after a minute or so. Another said she was very calmed by my voice singing along with the machine.

Continuing the theme of sound frequency healing, I sounded my 528hz wah wah gong, and let the clear resonant note go on until it slowly faded to silence. This is said to be the Love Vibration, and it is credited with performing miracles and renewing DNA. It is also used as a diagnostic tool to assess chakra energies, and the level of harmony and discord in the body, energetically speaking.

I told the group about the time, during my sound healing training, this 528 frequency was used on a horse, as an energetic diagnostic tool. We all heard the frequency note dip as the tutor passed it over the horses' back leg. It turned out that particular leg had an injury caused by stumbling into a rabbit hole.

When I asked for a volunteer to demonstrate the 528hz frequency, a young woman eagerly came forward. I sounded the frequency and passed the wah wah gong up and down her body about a couple of inches away.

Everyone noticed a change in the frequency sound at her lower back. She then told us she was undergoing hospital treatment for chronic back pain. I expected a reaction from the group, but I am beginning to learn they are not usually very demonstrative or verbally expressive on matters of this kind.

I also noticed a change in the sound as it passed over her heart area. From experience, I have found this can mean the carrying of some deep emotional pain, which she confirmed. However, I was careful to respect her confidentiality in this matter.

It was now time for tea, and we finished the session with a blessing for peace and harmony for all beings and three rings of the Tingsha bells. All sound tends towards silence.

Members of the group are not used to discussing subjects like meditation and sound healing and said very little about them when having tea afterwards, preferring to speak of upcoming events. Yet they appear to enjoy the session.

This is a lesson for me in the practice of having no expectations of particular outcomes that I may be personally attached to.

Their approach is in sharp contrast to my meditation groups in Hebden Bridge, a creative alternative town in West Yorkshire, who readily discuss with interest the effects of sound frequencies, and the esoteric philosophical aspects of silence.

There are different and contrasting cultures between Hebden

Bridge and Burnley. The former is generally an artistic and spiritual, alternative culture, and the latter is generally less well formally educated. This is not to be equated with either lack of intelligence or wisdom. The Vanguard community members have a knack of summing up what is happening in a succinct, perceptive, and common-sense way. They also express their feelings candidly and honestly.

This is the eloquence of England's working class people who can sum up a situation in a few expressive words that could take a highly educated journalist several thousand words and still not express the heart of the matter so accurately.

Burnley is a traditional town where it would be foolish to overlook the fact that there are people here with great intelligence, entrepreneurial acumen, and all sorts of natural abilities that in some cases have never been identified or nourished. They need the opportunities for these qualities to come into the light and shine. Once I asked a young boy in a disadvantaged area of Burnley, "What do you want to be when you grow up?" He answered in a matter-of-fact way.

"Me? I ain't gonna be nothing."

I would encourage the development of community meditation groups as an extension of your practice should you wish to, for the undoubted benefits that can be brought to stressed and disadvantaged communities, alongside the many other necessary actions to support and regenerate such areas.

We were fortunate that the steam cleaning ceased in time for us to sit in silence together for a further few minutes before the end of the session. Afterwards, an elderly lady, N, came and told me she had recently had a painful hospital procedure as a test of the health of the colon and the medics had offered her gas and air to assist her tolerance of the test. Finding no relief from the gas and air, she began meditation breathing as learned in our group. She told me she then felt no discomfort. N remarked 'I thought I would tell you as I knew you would be right suited.'

CONCLUSION

A path to happiness is essentially about letting go of the idea that you have to be perfect. Letting go of the idea that you have to have surmounted and conquered all your difficulties and problems before you can allow yourself to be happy. That is not true.

Happiness is within your grasp now. Maybe not all the time, maybe not completely but sometimes, and maybe often.

Our Achilles heels, our disorders, and persistent problems can go on for many years and can become powerful self-sabotaging mechanisms blocking our path to happiness.

For we can come to believe that we do not deserve to be happy if we still have areas of imperfection.

Let us blow that notion out of the water. It is not true.

The only impediment to our happiness is the way we feel about things.

We cannot afford to wait until we have reached a state of perfection before allowing ourselves to be happy. For on that basis we may end up denying ourselves the happiness we could have had all along.

It is enough for you to do your best, and at the same time you can remember to take the opportunity to laugh, love, and live life to the full.

It can be a simple thing like the wind in your hair or a beautiful view. Or being grateful for your sight, or for the ability to digest your food, or the feel of your dog's faithful silky head beneath your hand.

Look for the small things, the blessings all around and within us all the time. We discount these blessings so often and bypass joy.

It can be challenging, but can you seek the good within the seemingly bad experiences?

Maybe you could even feel enjoyment as you complain about something? Maybe you could sometimes laugh at yourself with a deep belly laugh?

Can there even be a flash of happiness or deep appreciation when you are ill?

This is not about forced, fake happiness. It is about seeking the yin yang balance in our experiences.

What makes you feel happy? Become aware of your sources of happiness and consciously avail yourself of them as long as they do not hurt you or anyone else.

Of course, be aware that some quick fix routes to happiness carry a sting in the tail and ultimately deliver unhappiness.

Happiness can be simply here and now. Just relax your shoulders, soften your eyes and your heart. Put a half smile on your face and call to mind a person who loves you. Allow that warm feeling to extend throughout your body.

Imagine a happy feeling is flowing over you and through you as if you are standing under a fountain of warm beaming golden light. Let any remaining tension flow out of you and dissolve into the earth.

Can you allow yourself to feel happy in the here and now, for this moment? Let your heart answer a delightful, delicious YES.

ABOUT THE AUTHOR

Kath Reade (B.Sc.Hons.MA. Cert.Ed.) Meditation teacher, Gong master, Singer-Songwriter, had a tough childhood and was a young carer for her chronically ill mother. A career at the frontline of social care, in social work and a professional teaching career followed. After being an elected councillor for some years she became the first woman Leader of Burnley Council. Kath was an international speaker on poverty and regeneration, as board member of the North West England Development Agency. She was Chair of Cumbria and Lancashire NHS Health Authority and East Lancashire NHS.

Kath has practiced meditation since the 1990s and in 2018 became a qualified meditation teacher. Her meditation practice is central to her life, as is her love of Qi Gong daily movement and music.

Kath has become a best-selling international author with 'Jumping Over My Shadow -The Travel Diaries of Kath Reade' and 'The Places That Call My Heart -Travels Through the British Isles'. These are available on Amazon Kindle.

Her books and CDs of her songs are loved by many, and can be found on YouTube and *kathreademusic.bandcamp.com* and her website *www.kathreade.co.uk*

Her music has been described as '...thoroughly feel-good and uplifting.' (Folkwords).

During the Covid pandemic Kath has been broadcasting her songs and writings, sound baths and meditations on Facebook Live. She has been acquiring thousands of views, followers, and messages from all over the world.

Kath is trained in Sound Healing by Tim Wheater and Don Conreaux and is a reiki master. Kath has a great following for her legendary gong sound baths based in Hebden Bridge, West Yorkshire.

> 'Kath Reade brings a wonderful warm insight to her unique work with sound. Endowed with an extraordinary voice and healing sensitivity, her abilities are a gift for humanity.' - Tim Wheater.
>
> "A live performance by Kath Reade is unmissable" -Tykes News.

Kath has been married to Paul, a retired computer professional for half a century, and their son Shaun (B.A.Hons.Soc., BACP) has his own IT company and counselling practice. He is a trained pianist, who loves to boat on Scottish lochs.

Contact Kath Reade at *www.kathreade.co.uk*

Printed in Great Britain
by Amazon

10644474R10064